Wildlife-Associated Recreation Trends in the United States

A Technical Document Supporting the Forest Service 2010 RPA Assessment

Miranda H. Mockrin, Richard A. Aiken,
and Curtis H. Flather

I0450461

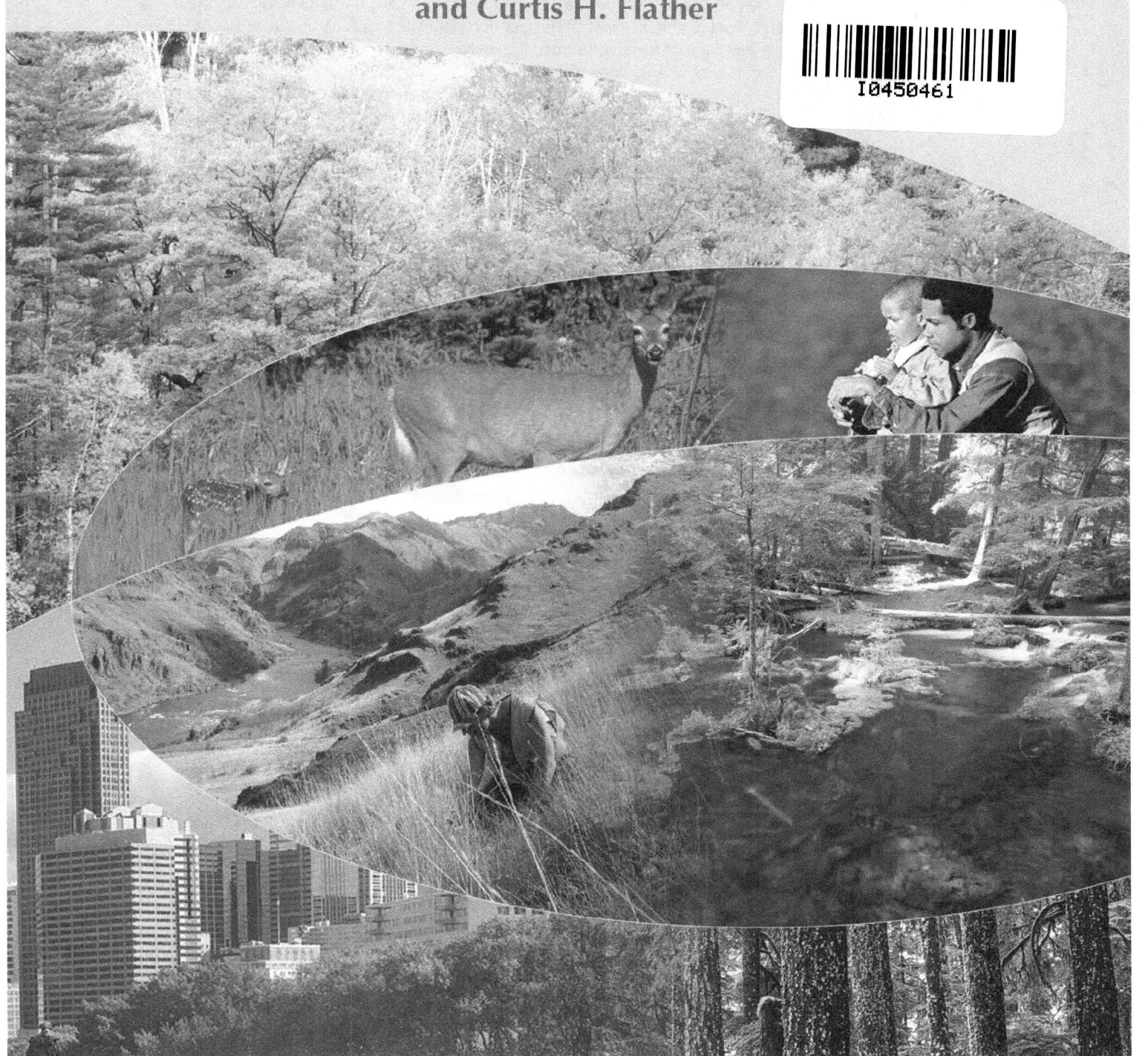

Abstract: The Forest and Rangeland Renewable Resources Planning Act (RPA) of 1974 requires periodic assessments of the condition and trends of the Nation's renewable natural resources. In this report, we document recent and historical trends in hunting and wildlife watching to fulfill RPA requirements. Using data from the U.S. Department of the Interior, Fish and Wildlife Service's National Survey of Fishing, Hunting, and Wildlife-Associated Recreation we present historical trends back to 1955 as well as recent changes from the past 10 to 20 years to evaluate changes in recreation since the 2000 RPA Assessment. We report on several attributes of wildlife recreation, including number of participants, days participating, recreation on public and private land, and economic expenditures. We found that participation in wildlife-associated recreation continues to change, with fewer Americans taking part in hunting and wildlife watching over the past 20 years. Total days devoted to recreation have declined along with number of participants, but the annual expenditures per participant and days of recreation per participant have generally risen or remained stable. We discuss variation in participation among types of hunting and across RPA Regions of the United States. Documenting and understanding these changes in wildlife-associated recreation is essential to ensure the continued successful management of wildlife resources.

Keywords: recreation, wildlife, hunting, wildlife watching, demographic trends

Authors

Miranda H. Mockrin is a Research Biologist at the U.S. Department of Agriculture, Forest Service, Rocky Mountain Research Station in Fort Collins, Colorado.

Richard A. Aiken is an Economist with the U.S. Fish and Wildlife Service in Arlington, Virginia.

Curtis H. Flather is a Research Ecologist at the Rocky Mountain Research Station in Fort Collins, Colorado.

Acknowledgments

This work was supported by the U.S. Forest Service Research and Development's Resources Planning Act research program as part of the Forest Service's national assessment reporting requirements mandated by the Forest and Rangeland Renewable Resources Planning Act. This report also fulfills, in part, the requirements of the Presidential Management Fellows Program for Miranda Mockrin. We also thank Dr. Susan Winter, U.S. Forest Service, Washington Office, Ecosystem Management Coordination, for her assistance in compiling participation and expenditure data associated with wildlife recreation on National Forests and Grasslands. This report also benefited from the constructive comments we received from Dr. Linda Langner, U.S. Forest Service; Dr. Erin Carver, U.S. Fish and Wildlife Service; Dr. Ken Cordell, U.S. Forest Service; and Dr. Richelle Winkler, Michigan Technical University.

Contents

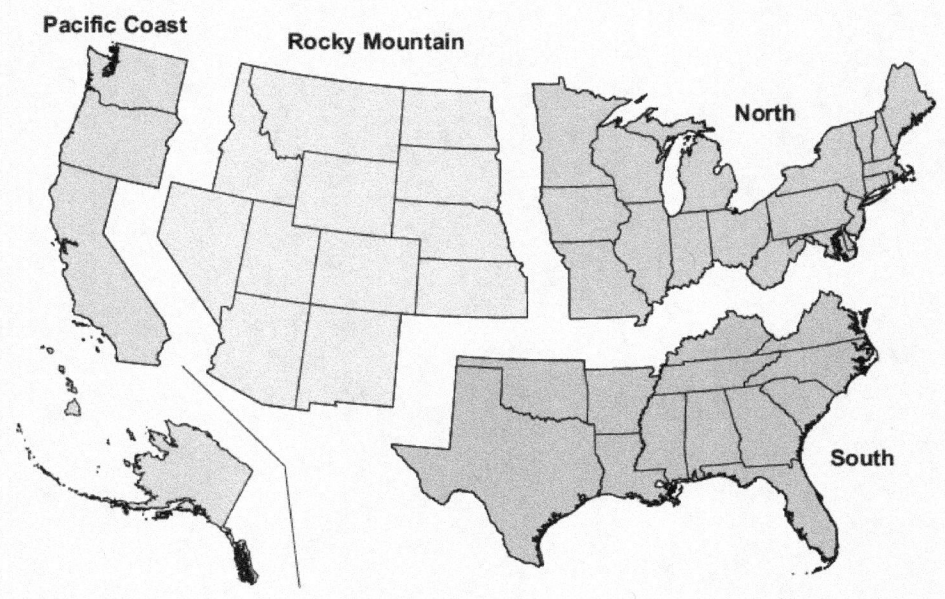

Introduction

Wildlife resources have long been directly used by Americans, providing substantial economic and nutritional benefits. Traditionally, views on wildlife resources were utilitarian and commodity oriented, but values about wildlife have diversified over the past several decades. For example, a recent survey showed that western United States residents were nearly evenly divided between traditional views focused on wildlife use and views that stressed mutual benefits and non-consumptive use (Teel and Manfredo 2010). Similar transitions away from utilitarian views have been noted across the United States (Butler and others 2003; Mankin and others 1999). Over the past several decades, there has been an increasing recognition of the broader ecosystems services provided by wildlife. Wildlife provides social and cultural benefits and plays a vital role in ecosystem functioning, including contributions to seed dispersal, pest control, and nutrient cycling (de Groot and others 2002; Duffy 2009).

In addition to these ecosystem services, hunting and wildlife watching make valuable contributions to local economies. According to the most recent national survey of wildlife-associated recreation, hunters spent $22.9 billion and wildlife watchers spent $45.7 billion on their respective activities in 2006 (USDI FWS and U.S. Census Bureau 2007). These direct expenditures provide insight into the economic benefits of recreation expenditures for local and regional economies, but they fail to account for the broader impact of these activities on the economy or their value to participants. For example, an analysis of the economic contribution of hunting revealed that the $22.9[1] billion spent by 12.5 million hunters in 2006 generated $66.0 billion in overall national economic impact, including supporting an estimated 600,000 jobs (Southwick Associates 2007). Similar economic contributions have been attributed to wildlife-watching expenditures (Williams 2010). In 2006, wildlife watchers, both at home and away from home, spent $45.7 billion in 2006 on direct expenditures for wildlife watching, generating $122.6 billion in wider economic output and supporting more than 1 million jobs (Leonard 2008).

Greater societal benefits, such as the physical and emotional well-being promoted by wildlife-associated recreation, are more challenging to quantify. The net economic benefit of each recreational activity has been proposed as a measure of this larger societal benefit and is estimated by measuring the amount a participant would be willing to pay, in excess of their direct costs, to participate in an activity. In 2006, hunters reported the net economic value of deer hunting in their home state as an average $657 per year per participant and the economic value of elk hunting at $523 per year (for more information on methodology, see Aiken [2009a]). For those who watched wildlife away from their homes, the net economic values were $407 per year per person for watchers participating in their state of residence (Aiken 2009a)[2].

---

[1] This estimate does not include an additional $11.7 billion spent on items that are used for both hunting and fishing.

[2] These economic measures are associated only with people who participate in these activities as a primary pursuit, and do not include other non-use values (for example, existence values, or the value reflecting the benefit people receive from knowing that a particular environmental resource exists).

The economic values associated with wildlife-based recreation make it important to document changes in recreation patterns, not only to anticipate economic impacts for local economies, but because many of the state agencies that manage wildlife and fish are funded primarily through revenues associated with hunting and fishing, such as licenses or excise taxes on firearms, archery equipment, and ammunition (Williams 2010). Nationally, licenses and taxes on hunters and anglers combined contribute an estimated 65 percent of state wildlife agency budgets (Mahoney 2009). Although there is growing interest in exploring different means of generating revenues from the broader public (Regan 2010), alternative funding sources are not yet widely used. Consequently, participation shifts in wildlife hunting will have significant impacts on the funds available for wildlife management (Jacobson and others 2010; Manfredo and others 2009).

Understanding how wildlife-associated recreation is changing along with socio-demographic change and how these shifts will affect management of resources and wildlife communities is essential to ensure science-based policy and informed decision making (Organ and others 2010). This philosophy was formalized by the Forest and Rangeland Renewable Resources Planning Act (RPA) of 1974 (P.L. 93-378, 88 Stat 475, as amended). The Act requires the U.S. Forest Service to prepare periodic resource assessments on the Nation's 1.6 billion acres of forest and range lands that report on (1) the current status and condition of resources based on an analysis of recent historic trends and (2) the future resource situation based on trend projections (Cortner and Schweitzer 1981; USDA Forest Service 2012). In support of the 2010 RPA Assessment, our goal is to provide an overview of recent historical trends in wildlife-associated recreation (hunting and watching) participation as a gauge on the demands for outdoor recreational activities that are directly dependent on wildlife resources. We also review some of the implications of these trends for the long-term management of wildlife resources and funding for management. This synthesis is intended to help natural resource managers understand past and current trends in recreation and resources, and anticipate future changes. Trends in fishing recreation and fish populations are summarized in a separate RPA document (Loftus and Flather 2012). Projections of participation in hunting and fishing recreation are covered by Bowker and others (2012).

To assess recreation trends, we use data gathered by the National Survey of Fishing, Hunting, and Wildlife-Associated Recreation (FHWAR), funded by the U.S. Fish and Wildlife Service. Among the different activities covered by the survey, we focus on wildlife watching, all hunting, and three subsets of wildlife hunting: big game, migratory birds, and small game[3]. We report mostly on wildlife watching that occurs away from (>1 mile) the home (also referred to as nonresidential wildlife watching) because it is an indication of outdoor recreation by individuals whose primary purpose is to view, feed, or photograph wildlife. Primary purpose means that for both hunting and wildlife watching, the participant's central aim must be the wildlife-associated recreation activity. Data for unplanned hunting or wildlife watching while on trips taken for another purpose were not included in FHWAR. We also separately report broad trends in wildlife watching that occurs around the home (also referred

---

[3] FHWAR has a fourth subcategory of hunting, other animals. We do not report on other animals, but this type of hunting is included in the broader all hunting category.

to as residential wildlife watching) to provide a more complete picture of the importance of wildlife watching to the American public. We provide more background information about FHWAR in the Methods section. A glossary is provided at the end of the document to define terms we use throughout this report.

Methods

From 1955 onward, wildlife-focused recreation activities have been monitored by FHWAR, the longest running and most detailed record of the American public's participation in hunting and wildlife watching (watching was added in 1980)[4]. In this section, we present some background information on FHWAR methods and administration, and then review the methods we used to document the trends reported in this document.

FHWAR Methods and Administration

As a survey, FHWAR creates estimates of number of participants, days, and expenditures by interviewing a portion of the American public. A full census of recreationists would be impractical, so researchers sample a portion of the population and then generate estimates for the larger population. This approach contrasts with much of the information reported on hunting and fishing by individual states, which relies upon license data. All data reported are for recent recreation experiences (within the past year) in which the participant's primary purpose was to hunt or watch wildlife.

FHWAR is administered in two stages. First, a broad screening phase is used to establish patterns of participation among the general public, concentrating on those aged 16 and older, while also obtaining basic information on those aged 6 to 15. A more comprehensive survey instrument is then used with those aged 16 and older who participated in wildlife-associated recreation in order to gather detailed information on activities and expenditures for the different types of hunting and wildlife watching. Expenditures are broken down into multiple categories, including trip-related expenditures, equipment expenditures, and other expenses (for example, magazines, membership dues, contributions, land leasing and ownership, licenses, stamps, tags, and permits). Estimates are then generated for the number of participants, how often and where they participated, type of wildlife encountered, and money spent on wildlife-related recreation. Researchers use statistical analyses to better understand the variation around estimates and to compare different populations. In general, the more interviews that feed into an estimate, the less variation around an estimate, so changes seen Regionally or at the state level often must be larger than those seen nationally in order to be deemed statistically significant. For more information on the survey's sample design, implementation, and analysis, please see Appendices C and D of the National Survey of Fishing, Hunting, and Wildlife-Associated Recreation (USDI FWS and U.S. Census Bureau 2007).

---

[4] National Recreation Survey (now the National Survey on Recreation and the Environment) also has a long history in tracking recreation (since 1960) and is used for the RPA to assess broader outdoor recreation trends (Cordell 2012).

Wildlife-Associated Recreation Trends for 2010 RPA Assessment

In this report, we summarize FHWAR information on wildlife-associated recreation, including number of participants, total days of participation, days spent recreating per participant per year, as well as information on economic expenditures and patterns of recreation participation on public and private land. We also provide information on recreation on Forest Service lands based on visitor monitoring conducted by the Forest Service (English and others 2002).

Although FHWAR has been conducted every five years from 1955 to 2006, for this RPA Assessment, we generally focus on data from 1991 onward because survey methodology changed in 1991, switching from a 12-month recall period to a 4-month recall period[5]. The four-month recall period has increased accuracy in participants' reporting of their activities (USDI FWS and U.S. Census Bureau 2007: Appendix C). In some cases, we adjusted information prior to 1991 to be comparable to survey information from 1991 to 2006 (see Table 1).

We also focus on changes observed after the 2000 RPA Assessment (Flather and others 1999), which include the 1991 and 1996 National Surveys of Fishing, Hunting, and Wildlife-Associated Recreation. We then compare these changes to those projected by Bowker and others (1999) for the last RPA Assessment to determine if observed changes in recreation conform with past expectations. It is beyond the scope of this document to examine in detail

Table 1. Characteristics and comparability of data from National Survey of Fishing, Hunting, and Wildlife Associated Recreation presented within this report (1955 onwards). Years that can be compared are written with a dash between them. A semicolon separates years that are not directly comparable.

Data	National	Regional (where activity occurred)
Number of participants[a]		
Hunters	1955-2006, age 16+	1980-2006, age 16+
Big game/small game/migratory bird[b]	1955-2006, age 16+	1980-2006, age 16+
Wildlife watching (nonresidential)	1980-2006, age 16+	1985, age 16+; 1991-2006, age 16+
Number of days		
Hunters	1955-1970, age 12+; 1975, age 9+; 1980-1985; 1991-2006, age 16+	1980-1985, age 16+; 1991-2006, age 16+
Big game/small game/migratory bird[b]	1955-1970, age 12+; 1975, age 9+; 1980-1985; 1991-2006, age 16+	1980-1985, age 16+; 1991-2006, age 16+
Wildlife watching (nonresidential)	1980-1985, age 16+; 1991-2007, age 16+	1991-2006, age 16+

[a] For the data on number of participants, pre- and post-1991 data have been adjusted for this report to be comparable, except for wildlife watching at the Regional level.
[b] Waterfowl hunting data is available from all surveys. Dove hunting was added to the waterfowl hunting category in 1975, and the new grouping was termed "migratory bird hunting."

---

[5] Note that survey data from 1975 gave higher estimates than previous and subsequent surveys due to the use of mail-based, self-administered surveys. All other surveys have been conducted via telephone or in person.

the potential causes for any deviations in the recently observed participation patterns and those projected to occur by the previous RPA Assessment. However, we highlight cases of substantial deviation in order to identify opportunities for future research that may help disentangle the many potential causes for these deviations (for example, changing natural resource conditions, changing recreational preferences, methodological artifact).

Where data availability permits, we report on hunting and wildlife watching activities on not only the national scale but over each of the four RPA Assessment Regions (Figure 1). Each of these broad Regions differs in the types of ecosystems supported, the pattern of land use activity, and the demographic, economic, and social contexts within which natural resources are managed (USDA Forest Service 2012). The largest human populations are found in the North and South Regions (Table 2), while the Rocky Mountain and Pacific Coast Regions contain less than half of the North Region's population. Contrastingly, population growth rates from 1996 to 2006 were highest in the Rocky Mountain Region (26 percent), followed by the South (17 percent) and Pacific Coast Regions (15 percent) (Table 2). Because the number of potential participants varies greatly among RPA Regions, we report number of participants relative to a Region's population and days of participation for each activity to facilitate comparisons among Regions.

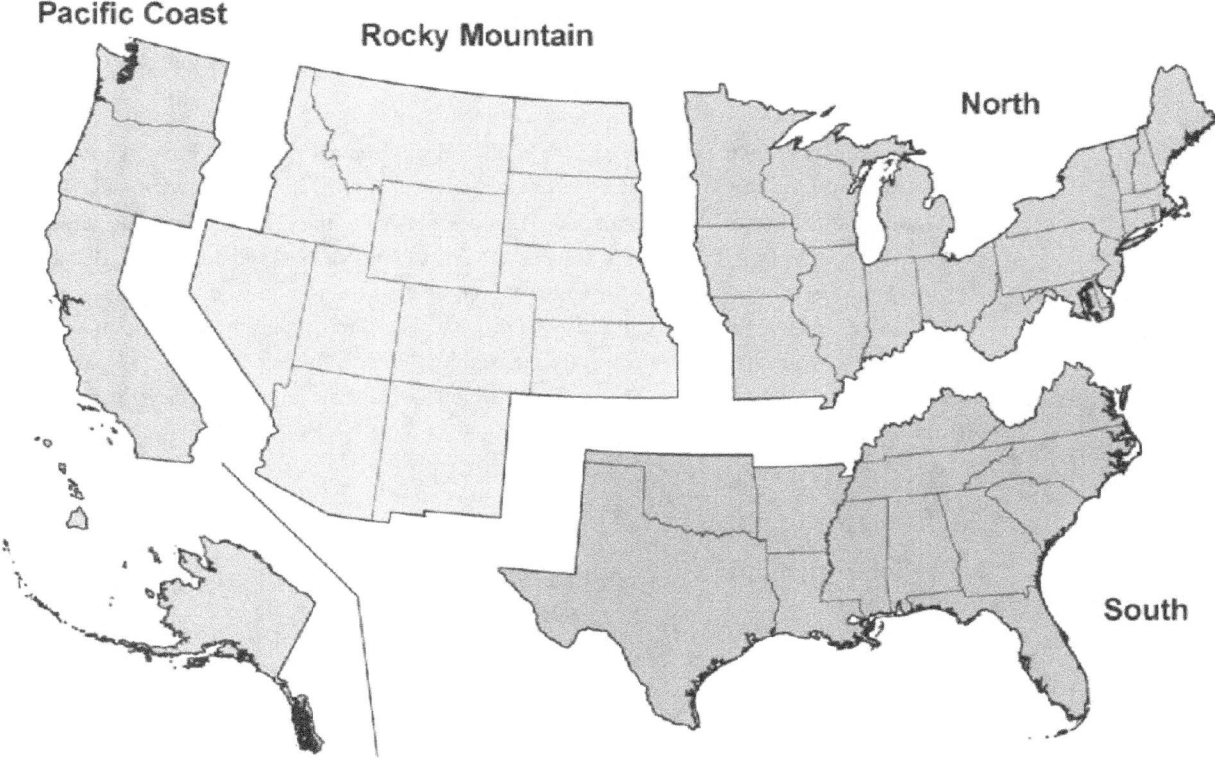

Figure 1. Forest Service RPA Assessment Regions.

Table 2. Population by RPA Region. Population (that is, age 16 and older, civilian, and noninstitutionalized) in the thousands, from the National Survey of Fishing, Hunting, and Wildlife-associated Recreation.

	1991	1996	2001	2006	Percent increase from 1996-2006	Average percent annual growth (1996-2006)
United States	189,964	201,472	212,298	229,245	13.8%	1.30[a]
North	86,418	89,076	90,692	95,700	7.4%	0.72
Pacific Coast	30,043	32,037	34,498	36,681	14.5%	1.36
Rocky Mountain	14,192	16,083	20,154	20,230	25.8%	2.32
South	58,839	65,177	66,528	76,201	16.9%	1.57

[a]This percent annual growth exceeds the 1.19% annual growth in U.S. population from 1995 to 2005 reported in USDA Forest Service (2012), but we note that our population is a subset of the total Census population reported in USDA Forest Service (2012).

For Regional estimates, the number of participants may include some people who have traveled from a home outside of the Region to participate. A wildlife hunter or watcher who participated in more than one Region was counted in each. We adjusted the data to avoid double-counting those who hunt wildlife in more than one state in a Region. Participation within a Region was selected as our reporting measure after examining participation by Region of residency (for example, all hunting conducted by residents of the North Region, regardless of where hunting occurred). We found that number of participants and days of participation categorized by the Region where recreation occurred gave similar trends to those estimated by Region of residency. However, we focused on hunting and watching by the location where the activity occurred because this measure represents the recreation pressure on the wildlife resource.

When possible, we provide estimates of the statistical significance of changes observed in recreation patterns at the 95% confidence level. Statistical significance was determined by calculating standard error of the estimated difference between time periods, following standard methods for FHWAR (USDI FWS and U.S. Census Bureau 2007, Appendix D). Because Regions have fewer residents than the entire nation, relative changes must often be larger than national changes to be deemed statistically significant. The same pattern holds true among Regions: those with smaller populations (for example, Rocky Mountain and Pacific Coast) must experience relatively larger changes in participation patterns to result in statistically significant changes.

Results and Discussion

National Participation in Hunting and Wildlife Watching

Hunting

Over the past 50 years, the total number of hunters varied, growing from 1955 to 1975, slowly declining through 1996, then showing a greater decline over the past 10 years (Figures 2a, 2b). In comparison to overall population levels in the United States (Figure 2b), increase in the number of hunters exceeded or closely tracked total US population growth up to 1980,

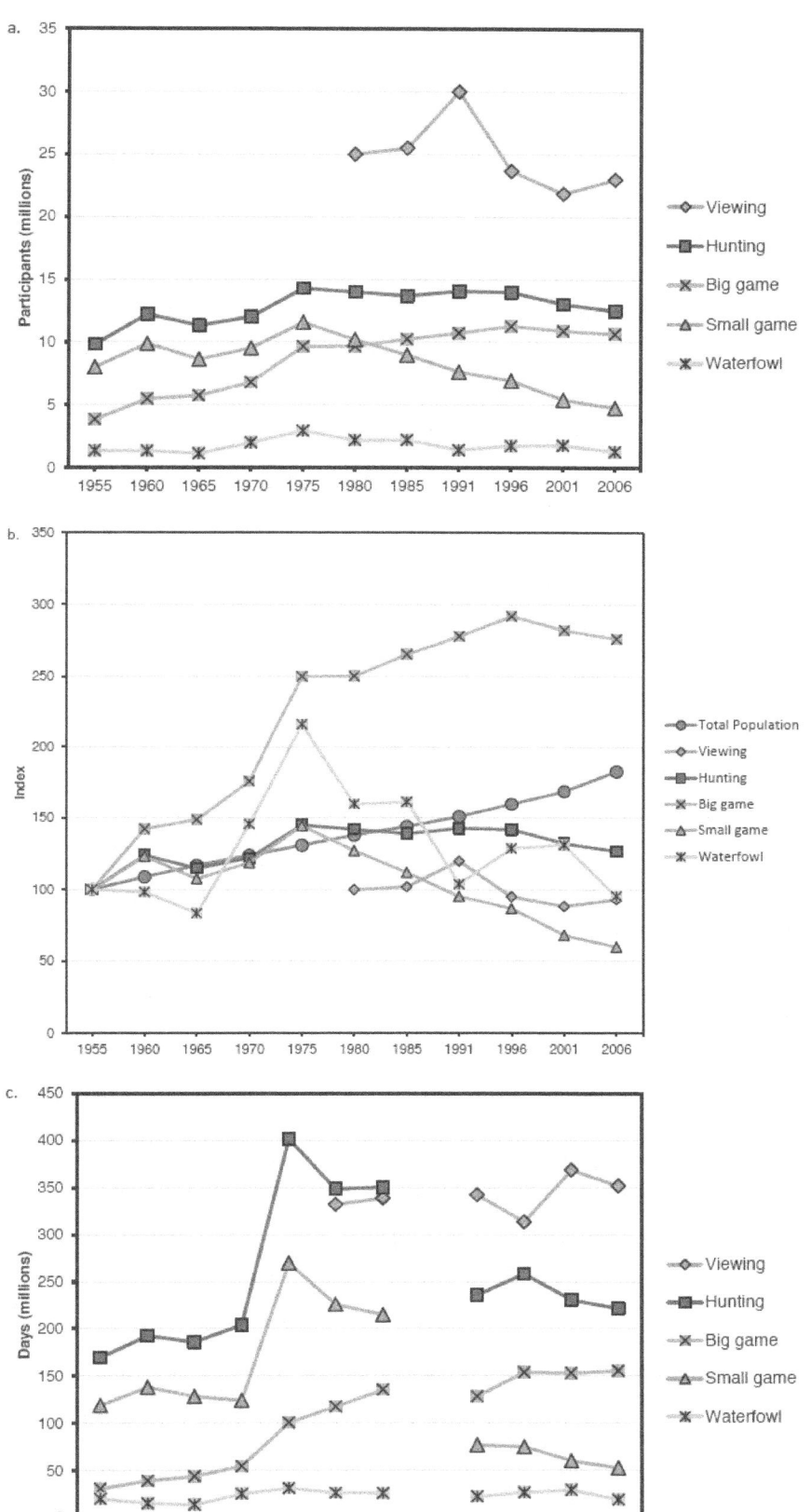

Figure 2. (a) Number of participants in wildlife hunting and nonresidential wildlife watching from 1955 to 2006. (b) Indexed number of participants shows change for each activity and the U.S. general population (age 16 and older) relative to the starting value (1980 for viewing, 1955 for other activities). (c) Trends in the number of days that persons spent participating in recreational activities dependent on wildlife. The break in the data on days from 1985 to 1991 reflects changes in survey methodology. Data before 1985 are comparable, as are data after 1991. See Table 1 for ages used in figures. See Aiken (2009b, 2010) for more information on participant trends from 1955 to 2006.

Table 3. National participation rates (percent of the population 16 years old and older) in wildlife recreation activities from 1991 to 2006. Changes in participation from 2006 to 1996 are expressed both in relative and absolute change.

	1991	1996	2001	2006	Absolute change (2006-1996)	Relative change ([2006/1996]/1996)
Hunting	7.5%	6.9%	6.1%	5.5%	-1.40%	-20.3%
Big game	5.7%	5.6%	5.1%	4.7%	-0.90%	-16.3%
Small game	4.1%	3.4%	2.6%	2.1%	-1.30%	-38.2%
Migratory bird	1.6%	1.5%	1.4%	1.0%	-0.50%	-33.3%
Wildlife watching	15.9%	11.7%	10.3%	10.0%	-1.70%	-14.5%

after which the number of hunters did not keep pace with growth in the US population. From 1991 to 2006, the percentage of the U.S. population that reported engaging in any kind of hunting has declined steadily from 7.5 percent of the total population to 5.5 percent (Table 3). The number of days spent hunting followed a similar pattern to the number of participants—increasing through 1975 but declining over the past 10 years (Figure 2c). For all hunting combined, the decline in days was steepest from 1996 to 2001 (a significant 11 percent decline) and then lessened by the next survey with a nonsignificant 4 percent decline from 2001 to 2006. The annual number of days devoted to hunting per participant rose from 1991 to 1996 and then declined slightly, remaining stable at approximately 17.5 days per person in 2001 and 2006 (Table 4). The most notable changes since the 2000 RPA Assessment (based on 1996 data) were the significant 10 percent decline in the number of hunters and the 14 percent decline in the total number of days spent hunting. Because the number of days spent hunting per participant has been stable over this time period, the decline in total days spent hunting over the past two surveys is a direct result of the decline in participants.

Patterns of participation among types of hunting activity (small game, migratory bird, and big game hunting) varied over time (Figure 2). Among small game hunters, the number of participants generally tracked the total number of hunters and general population through 1975; after which, there was a steep decline in the number of participants. By 2006, the number of small game hunters had declined 66 percent from the peak number of participants in 1975. Set against a backdrop of increasing U.S. population, national per capita participation in small game hunting has shown a monotonic decline since 1991, with the participation rate declining by 1.3 percentage points since 1996 (Table 3). The number of days devoted to small game hunting have also declined, decreasing by more than 25 million days nationally since 1991, with most of the decline occurring since 1996 (Figure 2c). Since the 2000 RPA Assessment, number of participants and total number of days for small game hunting have declined by more than 30 percent (Table 5). Similar to all hunting, the decline in days follows from the decrease in participants because the number of days spent pursuing small game per hunter remained relatively steady (11 days per hunter) from 1996 to 2006 (Table 3).

The number of migratory bird hunters also declined after the 1970s. By 2006, the total number of participants was less than the number recorded in 1955, with 1 percent of the U.S. population in 2006 participating in migratory bird hunting (Figure 2). The number of days spent hunting migratory birds remained steady through the 1970s and 1980s and showed statistically significant increases from 1991 through 1996 (19 percent). The average number

Table 4. Average number of days per participant in wildlife-associated recreation activities estimated nationally and by RPA Region (see Figure 1).

Activity/Region	1991	1996	2001	2006	Change since last RPA Assessment (=2006-1996)
All hunting					
National	16.8	18.4	17.5	17.6	-0.8
North	16.7	17.2	16.7	16.9	-0.3
South	18.5	21.3	19.7	19.6	-1.7
Rocky Mountain	10.7	12.2	12.1	11.2	-1
Pacific Coast	12.0	15.4	12.7	12.2	-3.2
Small game					
National	10.1	10.8	11.1	10.9	0.1
North	10.5	10.7	11.4	11.2	0.5
South	10.1	11.2	11.5	11.2	0
Rocky Mountain	7.9	9.7	8.5	8.7	-1
Pacific Coast	8.0	9.7	7.3	8.7	-1
Migratory birds					
National	7.4	8.6	9.9	8.6	0
North	8.6	9.2	9.5	8.5	-0.7
South	7.0	7.1	9.2	8.1	1
Rocky Mountain	6.2	8.7	8.6	7.0	-1.7
Pacific Coast	6.5	10.9	12.5	7.9	-3
Big game					
National	12.0	13.6	14.0	15.4	1.8
North	11.0	12.2	12.5	12.7	0.5
South	14.5	16.9	17.2	17.8	0.9
Rocky Mountain	7.7	8.5	8.6	9.0	0.5
Pacific Coast	9.8	11.0	10.8	11.8	0.8
Wildlife watching					
National	11.4	13.3	17.0	15.3[a]	2.0
North	8.7	9.9	16.4	12.1	-4.3
South	7.9	9.3	11.4	11.3	-0.1
Rocky Mountain	7.3	8.7	9.4	8.3	-1.1
Pacific Coast	10.4	11.3	10.5	13.4	2.9

[a]National estimate exceeds Regional estimates because participants who watched wildlife in multiple Regions were counted only once in the national totals.

of days per year spent hunting migratory birds by participants has increased by slightly more than one day from 1991 to 2006 (that is, 7.4 days per hunter in 1991 and 8.6 days per hunter in 2006) (Table 4). The average number of days devoted to migratory bird hunting per year has consistently been smaller than days devoted to other wildlife recreation activities (Table 4). Since the 2000 RPA Assessment, the number of participants declined by a significant 25 percent. Over this time period, the total number of days devoted to migratory bird hunting also declined by a significant 25 percent. Similar to other types of hunting, because the number of days devoted to migratory bird hunting per participant annually has not declined, the decrease in total number of days is a result of the declining number of hunters.

In contrast to the other subcategories, big game hunting showed sustained growth in number of participants over time, increasing from 1955 through 1996 at rates that exceeded the general growth in the U.S. population (Figure 2b), although the number of participants

Table 5. Statistical significance of changes in participants and days over surveys at the national level. Changes that are significant at the 0.05 level are noted in bold text.

| | Percent change during period | | | | |
| | 10-year periods | | 5-year periods | | |
Activity	1991-2001	1996-2006	1991-1996	1996-2001	2001-2006
Participants					
All hunters	**-7**	**-10**	-1	**-7**	-4
Big game	+2	-5	+5	-3	-2
Small game	**-29**	**-31**	**-9**	**-22**	**-12**
Migratory birds	-2	**-25**	+2	-4	**-22**
Wildlife watching	**-27**	-3	**-21**	**-8**	+5
Days					
All hunters	-3	**-14**	+9	**-11**	-4
Big game	**+19**	+7	**+20**	0	+7
Small game	**-22**	**-30**	-3	**-20**	-13
Migratory birds	**+32**	**-25**	**+19**	+11	**-33**
Wildlife watching	+9	+12	-8	**+19**	-5

remained stable over the last 10 years (nonsignificant 5 percent decrease) (Table 5). By 2006, the number of big game hunters was nearly three times greater than in 1955. Examining participation rates in this subcategory relative to the national population shows that rates have declined from 5.7 percent of the total population in 1991 to 4.7 percent in 2006, a relatively small decline in participation rates when compared to other activities (Table 3). The total number of days devoted to hunting big game increased consistently through 1985 but has remained essentially stable over the past 10 years (Figure 2c, Table 5). Overall, the annual number of days of big game hunting per individual rose by more than three days from 1991 to 2006 (12.0 to 15.4) (Table 4). In summary, since the last RPA Assessment in 2000, the total number of big game hunters and days devoted to big game hunting were stable, with an average increase of 1.8 days devoted to big game hunting by each participant per year.

Wildlife watching

Participants in wildlife watching have only been surveyed from 1980 onward. During this time period, the number of nonresidential wildlife watching participants increased initially through 1991 and then declined (Figure 2a). By 2006, the number of individuals who watched wildlife away from home declined by 7 percent from initial 1980 levels. Most of this change in number of participants occurred from 1991-1996 (Table 3). The number of people who watch wildlife away from home has been stable from 1996 to 2006. National rates of participation in nonresidential wildlife watching declined over the past four surveys, from 15.9 percent of the total population in 1991 to 10 percent in 2006. The number of days devoted to nonresidential wildlife watching varied from survey to survey without a clear direction in trend. Days initially rose by a statistically significant 19 percent from 1996 to 2001 and then declined slightly from 2001 to 2006 (5 percent nonsignificant decrease). However, the annual number of days devoted to nonresidential wildlife watching per person has risen since 1991, from 11.4 in 1991 to 15.3 in 2006, an increase of nearly 4 days per year (Table 4), making this the highest increase in days per participant per annum for any wildlife-associated activity. In summary, since the last RPA Assessment, the number of nonresidential wildlife watchers and total number of days devoted to wildlife watching away from home have remained stable (nonsignificant decline of 3 percent and nonsignificant increase of 12 percent, respectively), while the average number of days devoted to wildlife watching per participant increased (Table 4).

Wildlife watching around the home followed the same general trajectory as wildlife watching away from home, with an initial rise followed by a decline and a final increase in 2006 (Figures 3a, 3b). Consistently more participants have reported watching wildlife around the home, and the most recent estimate in 2006 was greater than the starting value in 1980.

Regional Participation in Hunting and Wildlife Watching

Hunting

Examining trends for all types of hunting from 1980 through 2006, we found that the North and South Regions had the greatest number of people participating in hunting (Figure 4a), as well as the largest populations (Table 2). Although the Rocky Mountain Region has fewer residents (Table 2), there are relatively more people who report participating in wildlife hunting in the Region (Figure 4a); in contrast, in the Pacific Coast Region, there are relatively fewer participants but a larger overall population (Figure 4a). Because the reported number of

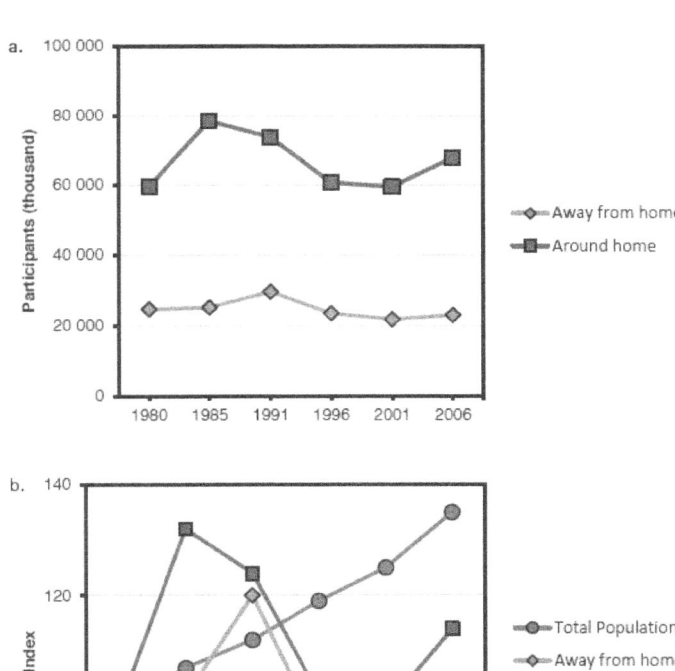

Figure 3. (a) Participants in wildlife watching from 1980 to 2006 (age 16 and over) among those who reported watching wildlife around the home and away from home (>1 mile from home) (b) Indexed number of participants shows relative change in each time period relative to the starting value in 1980 for wildlife watchers around the home and away from home and for the total U.S. population.

participants includes people who participate in a state but are not residents, this comparison between recreation and resident populations provides insight into the relative popularity of each activity but is not a means of comparing residents' relative rates of participation.

From 1991 to 2006, the number of hunters decreased in each Region, although the Rocky Mountain Region showed the least decline over time (Figure 4). Total days of participation have declined in the North and South Regions since 1991 and in the Pacific Coast and Rocky Mountain Regions since 1996 (Figure 4c). Among Regions, the North and the South had the highest annual number of days spent hunting per participant (17 and 20, respectively), almost more than a week per year higher than the Rocky Mountain and Pacific Coast Regions (12 and 11 days, respectively) (Table 4). For all Regions, days per participant in 2006 were greater than in 1991.

Focusing on the past 10 years of data showed a statistically significant decline in number of hunters and total days for the Pacific Coast Region (Table 6). All other Regions had statistically nonsignificant declines in number of participants and total number of days. Annual days devoted to hunting per participant declined in each Region from 1996 to 2006, with a small decrease in the North Region and a larger decline of more than three days per participant in the Pacific Coast Region (Table 4).

Similar to national patterns, Regional participation trends varied by hunting activity. For small game hunting, the greatest declines in number of participants from 1980 to 2006 were seen in the North and South Regions, with the smallest decline in the Rocky Mountain Region (Figures 5a, 5b). The total number of days spent small game hunting has declined across Regions but was relatively stable in the Rocky Mountain Region (Figure 5c). The average number of days each hunter devoted to small game per year increased for each Region since 1991. The North and South showed the highest number of days per participant per annum (11.2 for each in 2006), an average 2.5 more days per year than small game hunters in the Pacific Coast and Rocky Mountain Regions (Table 4). In summary, since the last RPA Assessment, there have been statistically significant declines of 26 percent or more in both number of participants and total days for the North, South, and Pacific Coast Regions. Only the Rocky Mountain Region did not experience a statistically significant decline, although decreases in both participants and days were seen there (Table 6). Despite these declines, the annual number of days spent hunting small game per participant remained relatively stable, with declines only seen in the Rocky Mountain and Pacific Coast Regions (decreases of one day per participant) (Table 4).

In the subcategory of migratory bird hunting, the South had the greatest number of participants (Figure 6a). The availability of wetland habitats for waterfowl likely contributes to this dominance in migratory game bird hunting. Forty-eight percent of the wetlands in the contiguous United States are found in the South (U.S. Department of Agriculture 2000). Since 1980, all Regions have experienced a substantial decline in the number of migratory bird hunters (from 40 to 50 percent; Figure 6b), but the South has maintained the greatest number of participants. The total number of days devoted to migratory game bird hunting declined in each Region from 1991 to 2006 (Figure 6c), with the greatest remaining number of days in the South. Examining the average days devoted to migratory bird hunting by participants

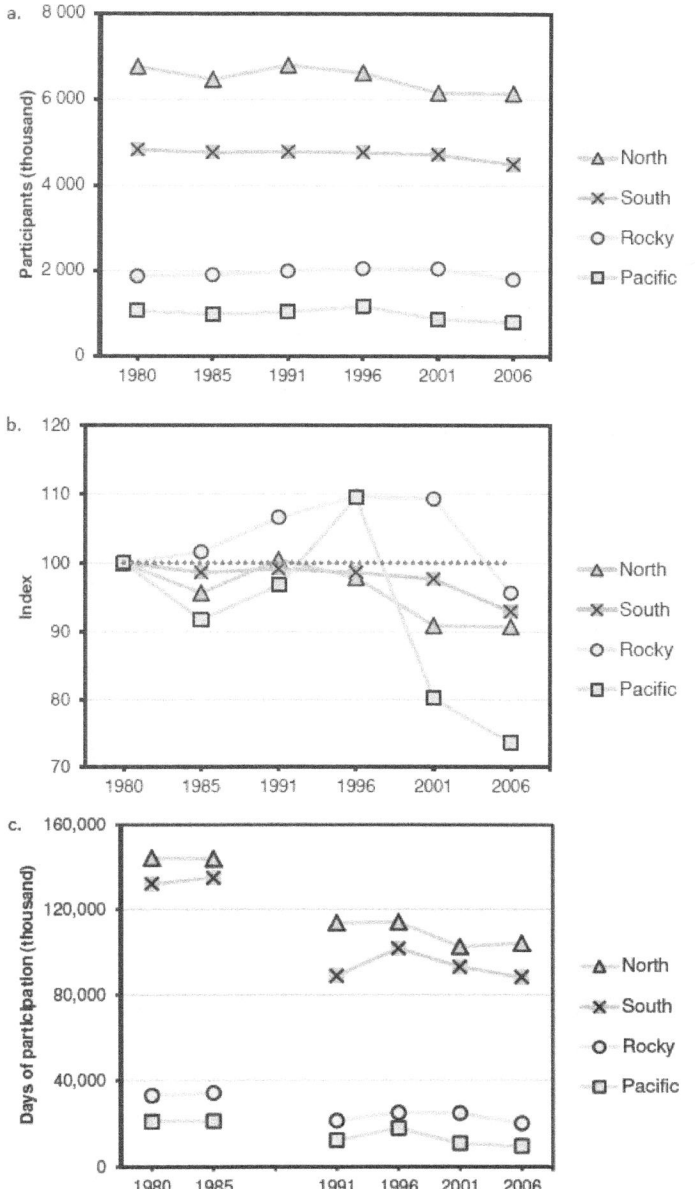

Figure 4. Regional trends for all hunting, including: (a) number of participants, (b) index of number of participants relative to the starting value in 1980, and (c) days. Indexed change in number of participants is included to provide a better measure of relative change within a Region. The break in the data on days from 1985 to 1991 reflects changes in survey methodology. Data before 1985 are comparable, as are data after 1991.

in 2006 reveals more parity between Regions (approximately eight days per participant for each Region; Table 4). From 1996 to 2006, the number of participants declined significantly in the North and the Pacific Coast Regions, with nonsignificant declines of 15 percent and 26 percent in the South and Rocky Mountain Region, respectively (Table 6). Total days devoted to migratory bird hunting declined in the North, Pacific, and Rocky Mountain Regions (statistically significant decrease of 32 to 60 percent), but total days remained stable in the South (Figure 6c, Table 6). Over this time period, the South was the only Region to show an increase in annual days devoted to migratory bird hunting per participant (Table 4).

Table 6. Statistical significance of changes in participants and days from 1996 to 2006 at the Regional level. Changes that are significant at the 0.05 level are noted in bold text.

Activity	Percent change 1996-2006	
	Participants	Days
All hunting		
North	-7.3%	-8.9%
South	-5.8%	-13.2%
Rocky Mountain	-12.7%	-20.1%
Pacific Coast	**-32.8%**	**-46.6%**
Big game hunting		
North	-2.3%	1.9%
South	0.6%	5.7%
Rocky Mountain	-13.3%	-7.8%
Pacific Coast	**-31.2%**	-26.0%
Small game hunting		
North	**-33.4%**	**-29.9%**
South	**-25.5%**	**-25.7%**
Rocky Mountain	-18.7%	-26.5%
Pacific Coast	**-51.7%**	**-56.7%**
Migratory bird hunting		
North	**-26.5%**	**-32.0%**
South	-14.6%	-3.2%
Rocky Mountain	-26.1%	**-40.6%**
Pacific Coast	**-46.6%**	**-61.5%**
Wildlife watching		
North	**-11.9%**	9.5%
South	-6.1%	12.2%
Rocky Mountain	9.6%	-0.4%
Pacific Coast	9.7%	30.6%

For big game hunting, Regional numbers of participants all increased until 1996 (Figures 7a, 7b). From 1996 to 2006, the South and North Regions were very close to no change, while the Rocky Mountain Region had a nonsignficant decrease of 13 percent and the Pacific Coast Region had a significant decrease of 31 percent (Table 6). When examining the total number of days spent on big game hunting in each Region, the South and the North both increased from 1991 to 2006 (Figure 7c), and the Rocky Mountain and Pacific Coast Regions showed more stable and lower numbers of days devoted to big game hunting (Figure 7c). The average number of days devoted to big game hunting per participant annually varied among Regions. In 2006, the South had the highest number of days (17.8), more than 5 days per year higher than in the other Regions (Table 4). Since 1991, the average number of days per participant grew for all Regions, with the highest increase in the South (3 days per year), followed by the Pacific Coast (2 days per year), the North (1.7 days per year), and the Rocky Mountain Regions (1.3 days per year). Since the 2000 RPA Assessment, the total number of participants in big game hunting declined significantly in the Pacific Coast Region, with no significant changes in other Regions. The total number of days devoted to big game hunting in each Region remained stable, while at the participant level, annual number of days spent big game hunting per person continued to grow.

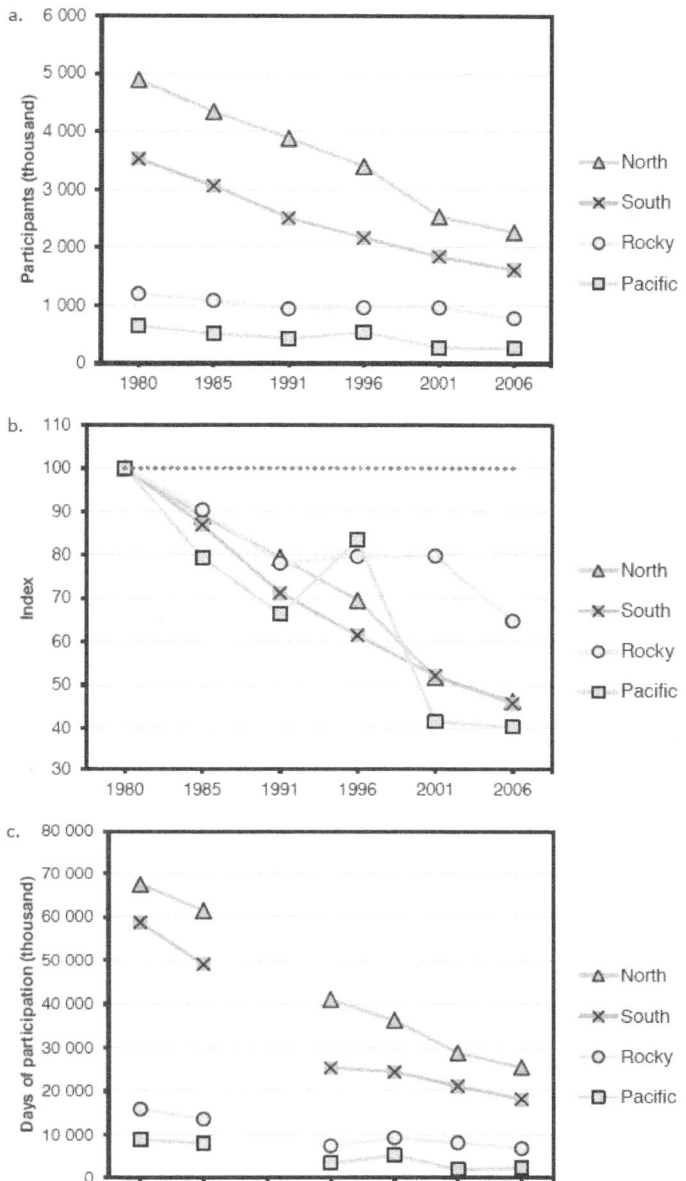

Figure 5. Regional trends for small game hunting, including: (a) number of participants, (b) index of number of participants relative to the starting value in 1980, and (c) days. Indexed change in number of participants is included to provide a better measure of relative change within a Region. The break in the data on days from 1985 to 1991 reflects changes in survey methodology. Data before 1985 are comparable, as are data after 1991.

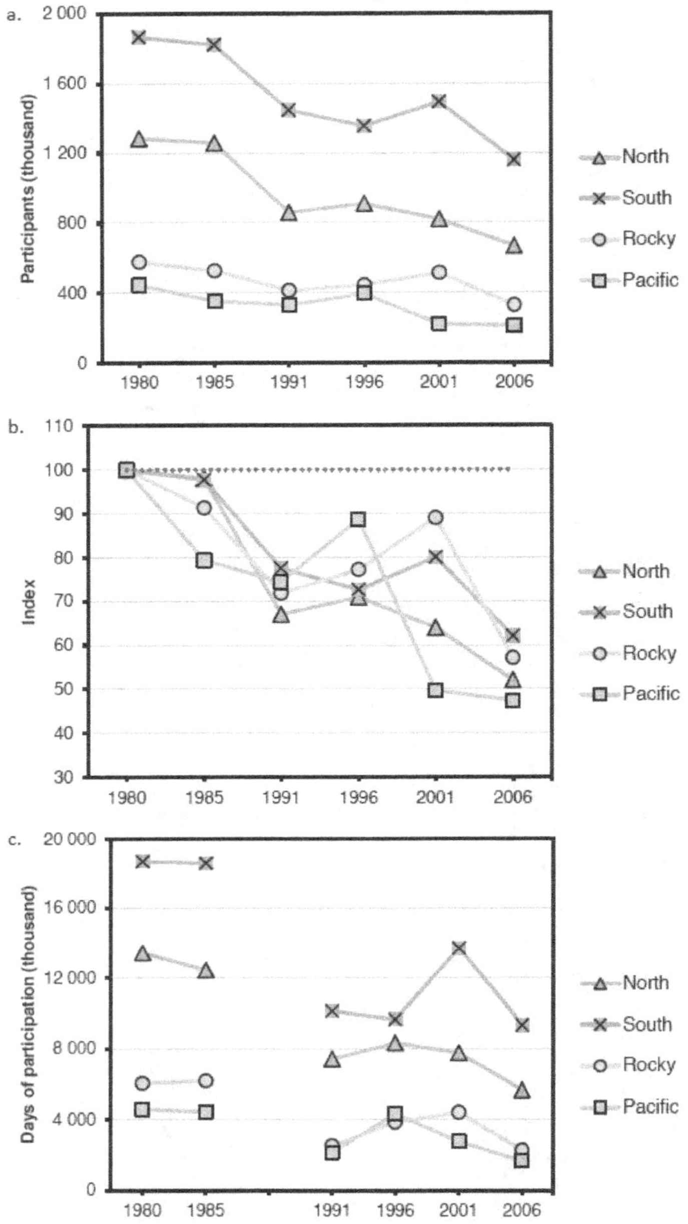

Figure 6. Regional trends for migratory hunting, including: (a) number of participants, (b) index of number of participants relative to the starting value in 1980, and (c) days. Indexed change in number of participants is included to provide a better measure of relative change within a Region. The break in the data on days from 1985 to 1991 reflects changes in survey methodology. Data before 1985 are comparable, as are data after 1991.

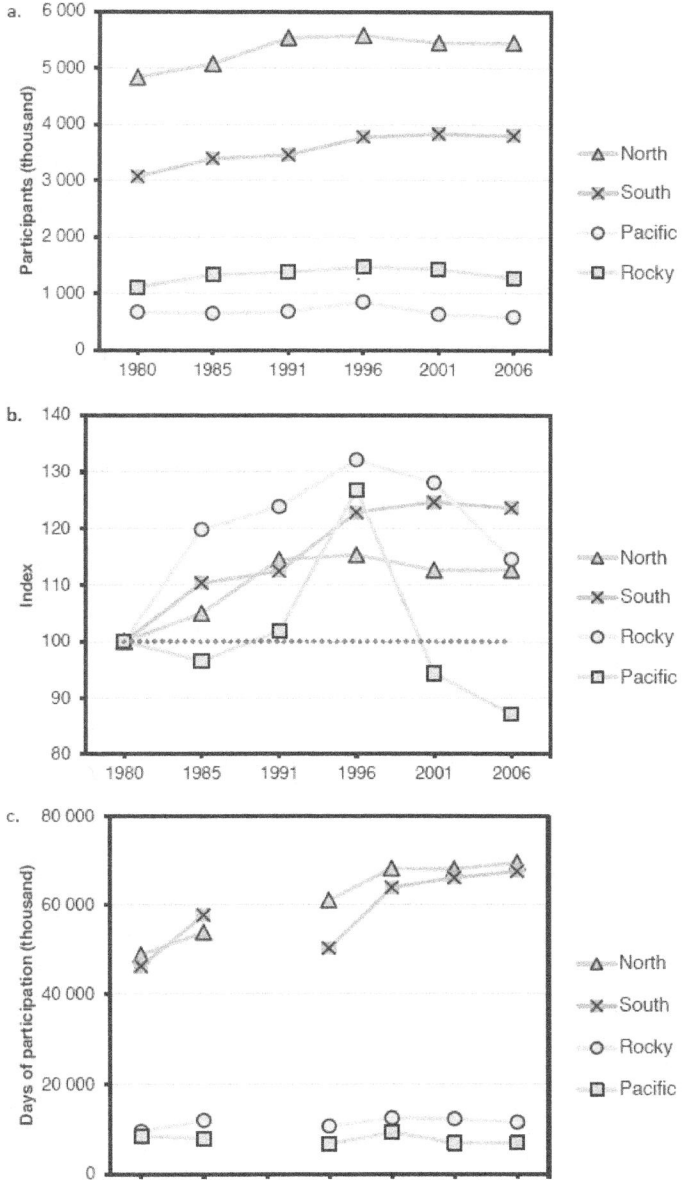

Figure 7. Regional trends for big game hunting, including: (a) number of participants, (b) index of number of participants relative to the starting value in 1980, and (c) days. Indexed change in number of participants is included to provide a better measure of relative change within a Region. The break in the data on days from 1985 to 1991 reflects changes in survey methodology. Data before 1985 are comparable, as are data after 1991.

Wildlife watching

Wildlife watching away from home initially declined in each Region after 1991 and then increased from 2001 to 2006 in all Regions except the North (Figures 8a, 8b). The Rocky Mountain and Pacific Coast Regions have roughly the same number of participants, making wildlife watching the only activity in which Rocky Mountain participation does not substantially exceed that of the Pacific Coast Region. However, the Rocky Mountain Region showed the most limited initial decline in number of wildlife watchers from 1991 to 1996 and the most positive overall trend in number of participants after 1996 (Figure 8b). The total number of days spent watching wildlife was stable or increasing for each Region from 1991 to 2006, with the Rocky Mountain Region having the smallest total number of days (Figure 8c). The average number of days spent watching wildlife per participant per annum increased for each Region since 1991 (Table 4). In 2006, the Pacific Coast Region had the greatest number of days per participant, closely followed by the North and South. The Rocky Mountain Region had notably fewer days of wildlife watching per participant (three days per year fewer than the South). When examining the period since the 2000 RPA Assessment, only the North Region showed a significant change in viewing participation with a 12 percent decline (Table 5). Total days showed nonsignificant increases in all Regions except the Rocky Mountain Region. The number of days per participant was higher in 2006 than 1991 for all Regions (Table 4).

Summary of variation among Regions

Regional patterns generally conformed to national trends without substantial variation between Regions. However, there were a few exceptions where individual Regions were unique from others. While the North Region generally had the highest number of participants in wildlife-associated recreation, followed by the South, the Rocky Mountain, and the Pacific Coast Regions, we noted two exceptions. The South Region had more migratory bird hunters than other Regions and was the only Region where total hunting days for migratory birds remained stable throughout the survey period. In the case of watching wildlife away from home, the Pacific Coast and Rocky Mountain Regions were nearly equal in the total number of nonresidential wildlife watchers (although the Pacific Coast had the smallest number of participants in all other wildlife-associated recreation). Among total days of wildlife watching, the Pacific Coast Region exceeded the Rocky Mountain Region.

Among other trends, all types of wildlife hunting generally declined in the Pacific Coast Region. From 1996 to 2006, both number of participants and days had statistically significant declines for all hunting combined, small game hunting, and migratory bird hunting. For big game hunting, only the number of participants declined significantly; the 26 percent decrease in number of days was not significant (Table 6). Among other Regions, the North and South showed some similar patterns from 1996 to 2006: they had similarly small changes in big game hunting participants, a similar decrease in small game hunting participants, and a similar increase in days spent hunting big game. However, these Regions were not always strongholds for wildlife-based recreation and trends sometimes differed. For example, the South was the only Region stable in migratory bird hunting and watching, while the North was the only Region to have a significant decline in wildlife watchers. The Rocky Mountain Region was unique because it was the only Region that did not decline significantly in days or participants

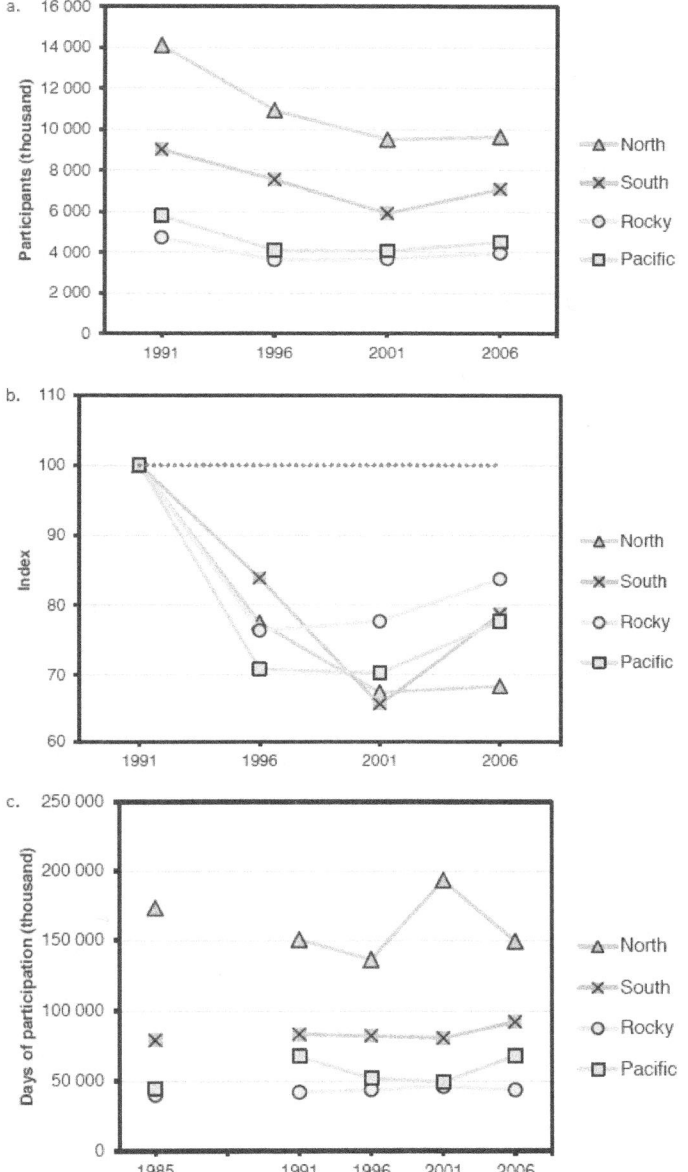

Figure 8. Regional trends for wildlife watching (away from home), including: (a) number of participants, (b) index of number of participants relative to the starting value in 1991, and (c) days. Indexed change in number of participants is included to provide a better measure of relative change within a Region.

of small game hunting over the past 10 years. Given the variability among Regions, it was difficult to infer any general pattern within Regions or activities. Further interpretation of these changes in recreation patterns will require understanding changes in wildlife resources in combination with demographic and socioeconomic factors at the Regional level.

Wildlife-Associated Recreation on Public and Private Lands

National patterns

Nationally, more than half of all hunters reported hunting on only private land in each survey from 1991 to 2006 (Figure 9). During the same time period, a stable 15 percent of all hunters reported hunting only on public land (Figure 9). Over this time period, there was a decrease in hunters using both public and private land (from a high of 29 to 30 percent in 1991 and 1996 to 24 percent in 2006) as hunters shifted to rely only on private land (Figure 9). In total, public lands hosted 54 million days of hunting in 2006 (25 percent of all hunting days), while 164 million days, or 75 percent of all hunting days, took place on private land (USDI FWS and U.S. Census Bureau 2007). In contrast to hunting, most nonresidential wildlife watchers pursued watching on public land. From 1991 to 2006, an average of 51 percent of all wildlife watchers used public land exclusively, 30 percent divided their time between public and private land, and 11 percent relied exclusively on private land (Figure 9). There are no discernible trends in public and private land use other than a growing number of respondents reported "unspecified."

Figure 9. Comparison of recreation occurring on public and private land for (a) wildlife hunting and (b) wildlife watching away from home from 1991-2006.

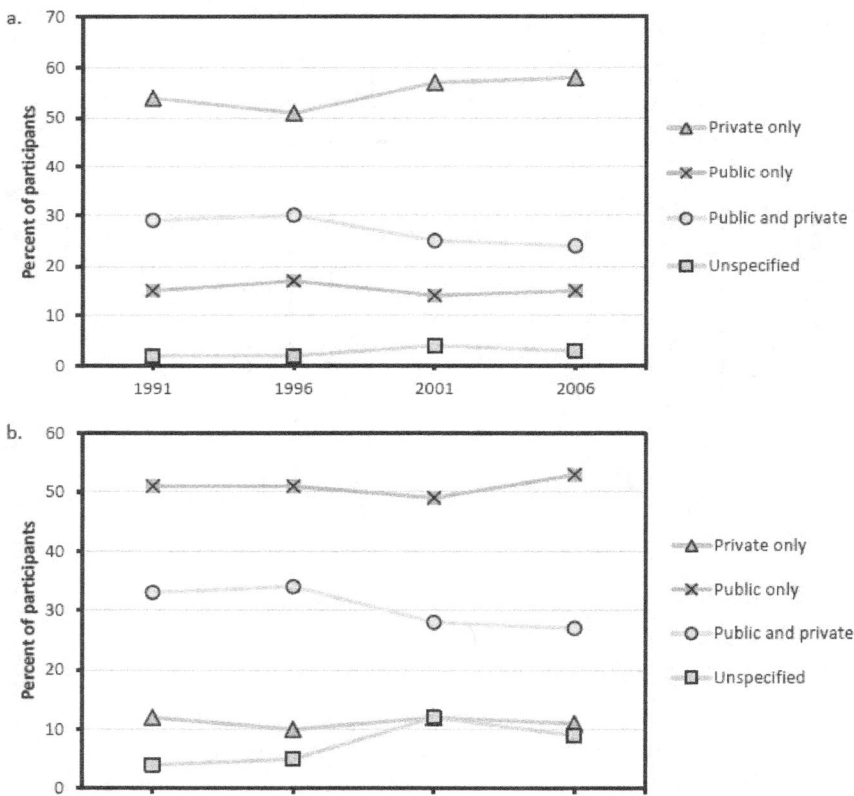

Regional patterns

For each RPA Region, we summarized the number of hunters and wildlife watchers who reported recreating on public and private land and excluded those who responded "unspecified" (Figure 10). Regional totals were adjusted to avoid double-counting within a Region, but individuals who participated in recreation in two Regions were counted in each. For each Region, we also estimated the relative availability of public and private land using the Protected Areas Database (PAD-US [USGS], version 1.1, http://www.protectedlands net/padus/preview.php). Public lands made up the largest relative area in the Pacific Coast Region due, in part, to the substantial public land area in Alaska (Figure 10). Public lands are also considerable in the Rocky Mountain Region (36 percent of total land area) but are much smaller in the North and the South (Figure 10).

Across all Regions, the vast majority of those who watched wildlife away from home reported recreating on public land, with slightly larger proportions recreating on public lands in the Pacific Coast and Rocky Mountain Regions. Hunters showed more Regional variation in public and private land use—low percentages of public land use were reported in the North and the South, but 50 percent or more of hunting participants reported using public lands in the Rocky Mountain and the Pacific Coast Regions. These results suggest that limited public lands in the North and the South lead to greater reliance on private lands for hunting. However, these relatively small proportions of public lands provide wildlife watching opportunities for a large number of people (following other Regional patterns, the North and the South have the greatest absolute number of wildlife watchers) (Figure 8).

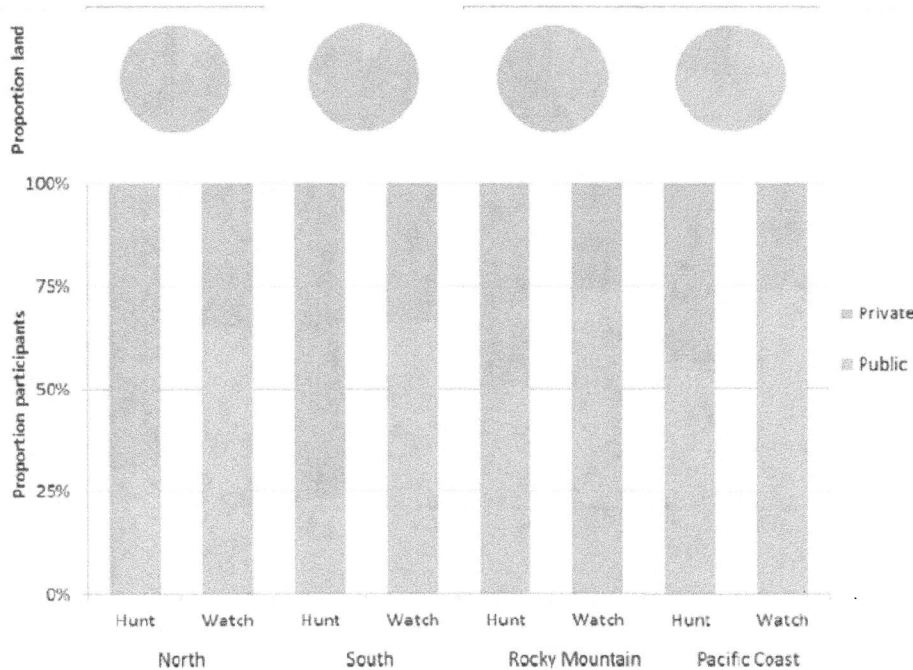

Figure 10. Proportion of participants in wildlife hunting and nonresidential watching on public or private land, as well as the distribution of land types in both areas, for 2006. Land area distributions from the Protected Area Database (PAD-US [USGS], version 1.1, http://www.protected-lands net/padus/preview. php)[1].

[1] Wildlife hunting is not allowed on all public land, although public lands do help preserve the health of wildlife populations. For each Region, the proportion of public land that does not allow hunting is: 1.2 percent (North), 2.0 percent (South), 5.8 percent (Rocky Mountain), and 12.3 percent (Pacific Coast).

Wildlife recreation on National Forest System lands

As public lands are nationally and Regionally important for wildlife-associated recreation, we wanted to further examine the specific contribution of National Forest System (NFS) lands. The NFS comprises 193 million acres on 155 National Forests and 20 National Grasslands. Most National Forest area is in the western United States (Table 7), but NFS lands are widely distributed so that 205 million Americans live within 100 miles of NFS land (Pam Froemke, personal comm.). The Forest Service has continuously monitored recreation activities, including hunting and wildlife watching, through a nationwide visitor use monitoring program since 2002 (English and others 2002). Results are reported in five-year increments, and we focus on the 2003 to 2008 results. Due to differences in methodology, results from the Forest Service's monitoring program cannot be directly compared to FHWAR data, but we present the most recent results here to provide specific information on the use of one type of public lands.

From 2003 to 2008, the Forest Service's national visitor monitoring program reported an annual 14.4 million visits to NFS lands for the primary purpose of hunting, with 2.3 million visits for wildlife watching (Susan Winter, personal comm.) (Table 7). Hunters reported a total of 9.7 million one-day visits and 16.6 million nights as part of overnight visits on NFS lands, while wildlife watchers reported 1.7 million one-day visits and 2.2 million nights as part of overnight visits on NFS lands (due to the methodology used, the number of days recorded from one-day visits and the number of nights recorded from overnight visits cannot be combined) (Figure 11). Total expenditures from these visits totaled almost $1.2 billion for hunting and $131 million for wildlife watching (estimated with expenditures on lodging, food, transportation, sporting goods, and souvenirs within 50 miles of the National Forest where the recreation took place) (Table 7). A detailed explanation of the expenditure profiles and how they were derived can be found in White and Stynes (2010).

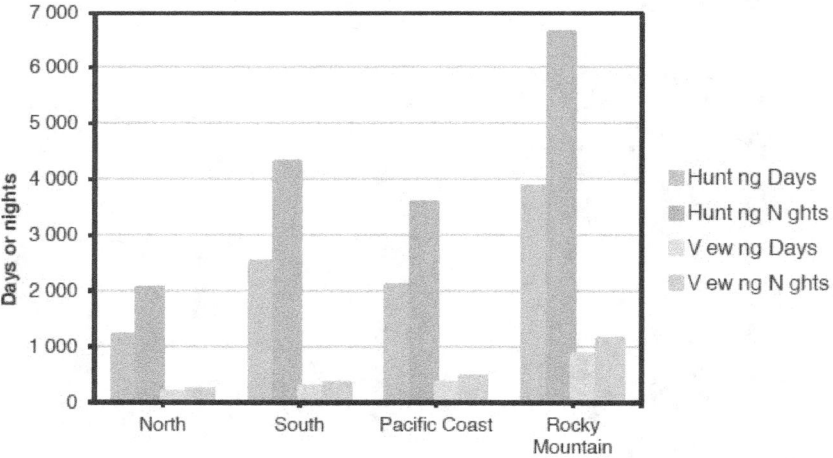

Figure 11. Days and nights spent hunting and wildlife watching on National Forests in 2008. Due to the methodology used, the number of days recorded from one-day visits and the number of nights recorded from overnight visits cannot be combined.

Table 7. Participation and expenditures on hunting and wildlife watching on National Forest System lands in 2008.

RPA Region	NFS land (km²)	% Total area	Hunting visits (million)	Hunting visit/km²	Hunting expend. (million)	Watch visit (million)	Watch visit/km²	Watch expend. (million)
North	62,483	8%	1.79	28.6	146	0.25	4.0	14.4
Pacific Coast	249,934	32%	3.12	12.5	255	0.49	2.0	28.2
Rocky Mountain	398,332	51%	5.77	14.5	472	1.17	2.9	67.8
South	70,294	9%	3.74	53.2	306	0.36	5.2	21.0
Total	781,043	100%	14.42	18.5	1179	2.27	2.9	131.0

Using the Forest Service's visitor monitoring data we can also group wildlife-associated recreation by RPA Region. The Rocky Mountain Region had the highest number of wildlife hunting participants, followed by the South and the Pacific Coast Regions, and far fewer hunters on NFS lands in the North Region (Table 7). Given the small size of NFS lands in the South Region, these lands received high amounts of use with an average 53.2 visits/km² followed by 28.6 visits/km² in the North Region (Table 7). Visitors who identified wildlife watching as the primary reason for their visit to NFS land were far less common than wildlife hunters but were still most common in the Rocky Mountain Region. The Pacific Coast Region had the next highest number of watchers, although still less than half that of the Rocky Mountain Region (Table 7). Because expenditures are calculated with a national estimate of expenditures per activity, expenditures per Region follow directly from the estimated number of participants. Similarly, Regional variation in the number of days and nights spent hunting and wildlife watching follow from the number of participants in each Region (Figure 11). Wildlife watching draws similar numbers of day and night visits, but night visits are more common for hunters (Figure 11).

National Economic Trends in Hunting and Wildlife Watching

We return to FHWAR data to examine national economic expenditures over time on wildlife-based recreation, including all hunting and wildlife watching. All values discussed are in 2006 United States dollars and are adjusted for inflation using the Consumer Price Index.

Hunting

Total economic expenditures on hunting have declined by approximately $3.5 billion since 1996, totaling $22.9 billion in 2006. Most of this decline occurred from 1996 to 2001 (-$2.9 billion), followed by a $600 million decline from 2001 to 2006. Annual participant expenditures have remained stable since 1996 at just over $100 per day spent recreating (Table 8). During this period, the average number of days devoted to hunting per participant remained stable, but the total number of days and hunters has declined, suggesting that the decrease in number of participants is driving the decrease in expenditures. FHWAR data on expenditures for owned or leased private land reveal that combined expenditures on land leased and owned for hunting have remained stable from 1991 to 2006, although there has been a decline in expenditures on land owned from 1996 to 2006 ($4.1 to $3.6 billion) and an increase in land leasing expenditures from 1996 to 2001 ($500 to $700 million) (Table 9).

Table 8. Economic expenditures on hunting and wildlife watching away from home. Methods for calculating economic expenditures have changed over the surveys, with additional items included in 1996 and 2001.

	1991	1996	2001	2006
Hunting				
Number of participants (million)	14.1	14.0	13.0	12.5
Total days (million)	236	257	228	220
Total amount spent (billion)	18.3	26.2	23.3	22.6
Amount spent per person	$1,301.29	$1,874.78	$1,787.60	$1,806.55
Amount spent per day	$104.59	$104.59	$102.20	$104.09
Wildlife watching away from home				
Number of participants (million)	30.0	23.7	21.8	23.0
Total days (million)	342	314	372	352
Total amount spent (billion)	17.7	23.4	31.1	30.8
Amount spent per person	$590.17	$985.74	$1426.90	$1337.53
Amount spent per day	$51.70	$74.40	$83.60	$87.40

Table 9. Expenditures on land leasing, land owned, and public and private land access fees for both hunting and wildlife watching (1991 to 2006).

	1991	1996	2001	2006
Hunting				
Public land access fees				
Total expenditures (thousands of dollars)	25,122	53,608	60,989	47,268
Number of spenders (thousands)	486	651	630	564
Percent of participants	3	5	5	5
Average per spender (dollars)	$51.69	$82.35	$96.81	$84.00
Private land access fees				
Total expenditures (thousands of dollars)	180,221	414,669	422,778	396,810
Number of spenders (thousands)	703	930	919	711
Percent of participants	5	7	7	6
Average per spender (dollars)	$256.36	$445.88	$460.04	$558.00
Expenditure land leased (thousands)	466,657	463,976	711,933	740,767
Expenditure land owned (thousands)	3,993,786	4,069,037	3,820,583	3,646,587
Wildlife Watching				
Public land access fees				
Expenditures (thousands of dollars)	192,354	222,360	130,887	140,508
Number of spenders (thousands)	5,870	5,865	3,879	4,331
Percent of participants	20	25	18	19
Average per spender (dollars)	$32.77	$37.91	$33.74	$32.44
Private land access fees				
Expenditures (thousands of dollars)	46,028	136,447	57,490	66,145
Number of spenders (thousands)	1,264	1,602	869	1,173
Percent of participants	4	7	4	5
Average per spender (dollars)	$36.41	$85.17	$66.16	$56.39
Expenditure land leased (thousands)	NA	(combined	343,487	316,166
Expenditure land owned (thousands)	NA	$1,712,850)	$5,084,065	$6,235,351

Fees associated with hunting on both private and public land may also provide some insight into wildlife recreation trends, although we note that only a small subset of hunters pay fees for land access on public or private land (approximately 5 percent pay for each land type) (Table 9). Over time, annual per person expenditures on private land access fees have more than doubled from $256 in 1991 to $558 in 2006. As per person fees rose, the number of hunters who reported paying private land access fees peaked at 930,000 in 1996 (7 percent of all hunters), declining to 711,000 people (6 percent of all hunters) in 2006 and generating just under $400 million. Annual per capita fees for public land are less than 20 percent of those for private land, and have been more stable in price, varying from $80 to $100 a person since 1996. Public land access fees generated less money than private land access fees, with $47 million paid by nearly 600,000 people in 2006 (Table 9). Fees paid for hunting on public land may include permits specific to hunting or fees required for access from all recreationists. Although the proportion of hunters paying public land use fees remained stable at 5 percent from 1996 to 2006, the total number of hunters doing so declined, following the general trend in number of hunting participants.

Wildlife watching

Total economic expenditures on wildlife watching (both at home and away from home) increased over the past four surveys ($26.8 billion in 1991, $35.3 billion in 1996, $41.2 billion in 2001, and $43.2 billion in 2006). FHWAR does not explicitly report economic expenditures for wildlife watching away from home, but by excluding all expenditures for watching at home (for example, bird feeders and plantings) and expenses that could have been used either at home or away from home (for example, cameras and binoculars), we generated conservative estimates of economic expenditures on wildlife watching away from home (Table 8). These values ranged from 66 to 75 percent of the total economic expenditures on wildlife watching and are likely underestimates of the true expenditures on wildlife watching away from home as they excluded expenditures that could be used either at home or away from home. Total amount spent on wildlife watching away from home grew from 1996 to 2006 by $7.4 billion, stabilizing at approximately $31 billion in 2001 and 2006 (Table 8). Variations in economic expenditures from 1991 to 2006 resulted from both changes in the total number of days devoted to wildlife watching and changes in the average amount spent per day by participants. Average amount spent per day has increased over the past four surveys, as has the amount spent per participant (Table 8).

Over the past four surveys, the percentage of wildlife watchers paying public land access fees has remained around 20 percent, with a peak at 25 percent in 1996. Over time, the number of watchers paying public land access fees has declined from 5.9 million in 1991 and 1996 to 3.9 and 4.3 million in 2001 and 2006, respectively (Table 9). Public use fees paid per person ranged from $32 to $38 annually (Table 9). Variation over time in number of fee payers has followed similar patterns for both private and public land access fees. Private land access fees paid per person rose from 1991 to 1996 but have been declining since then to $56 per person in 2006 (Table 9). With far fewer wildlife watchers paying private access fees, the total amount paid in private land access fees by wildlife watchers is less than half that paid for public land access fees by wildlife watchers.

When comparing wildlife watching and hunting, in 2006 the largest expenditure for land access fees was from hunters on private land ($397 million), due to the high per person prices. Many more wildlife watchers paid land access fees, but the total expenditures for wildlife watching on public land ($141 million in 2006) and private land ($66 million in 2006) were much smaller than national totals for private land access fees for hunting. While the 5 percent of watching participants paying fees is similar to the number of hunters who pay private land access fees, the annual fees are one-tenth of what hunters pay per capita in private land access fees (Table 9). Hunting on public lands in 2006 generated the smallest annual expenditure at $47 million.

Summary of Changes Since the 2000 RPA Assessment

The 2000 RPA Assessment included the 1991 and 1996 National Surveys of Fishing, Hunting, and Wildlife-Associated Recreation. Following, we highlight the changes that have occurred in the two National Surveys from 1996 to 2006 for hunting and wildlife watching at the national and RPA Region level. We then compare the changes seen in hunting and wildlife watching to those projected in the last RPA Assessment to determine if participation changes since the last RPA Assessment that have been documented here are occurring faster, slower, or at a pace consistent with past expectations. Expectations in the last RPA Assessment were derived from projection models that used the National Survey on Recreation and the Environment (NSRE) (Bowker and others 1999). Although the two national surveys differ (see Schuett and others 2009), we compared documented change (based on FHWAR) against projected change (based on NSRE) (Cordell 2004) on a relative scale. Projections developed for the last RPA Assessment were only for two broad categories of activities: all hunting and wildlife watching away from home, both at the national and Regional level.

Hunting—National

The most notable documented national changes in hunting since the 2000 RPA Assessment (1996 to 2006) were the significant 10 percent decline in the number of hunters and the significant 14 percent decline in the total number of days spent hunting (Table 6). These declines exceeded earlier projections based on a broader survey of all outdoor recreation (Bowker and others 1999) (Table 10). Bowker and others (1999) predicted a 4.8 percent decrease in all hunting participants at the national level from 1996 to 2006, while FHWAR showed a 10 percent decline over that period. Bowker and others (1999) also predicted a 2.6 percent decline in hunting days from 1996 to 2006, but FHWAR showed a decline of 14.3 percent over this time period. Combined, these findings suggest that the national decline in hunting participation may be occurring at a more rapid rate than was previously anticipated. However, we can't rule out methodological differences between the two surveys as an explanation for these deviations (see Walls and others 2009, p. 46).

Among different types of hunting, big game hunting remained stable in number of participants and days from 1996 to 2006. However, during this time period, participants and days devoted to small game and migratory bird hunting both declined significantly. Hunting expenditures decreased an insignificant 12 percent from 1996 to 2001 when the number of hunters also declined by 7 percent and then remained stable from 2001 to 2006.

Table 10. Projected and actual changes in hunting and wildlife watching participants and days for 1996 to 2006 with projections from Bowker and others (1999)[a] and actual change from the National Survey of Fishing, Hunting, and Wildlife-associated Recreation.

| | Hunting, 1996-2006 | | | | Wildlife watching, 1996-2006 | | | |
| | Predicted change | | Actual change | | Predicted change | | Actual change | |
	Participation	Days	Participation	Days	Participation	Days	Participation	Days
North	-2.2%	0.2%	-7.3%	-8.9%	6.2%	13.9%	-11.9%	9.5%
South	-12.4%	-8.3%	-5.8%	-13.2%	14.4%	20.6%	-6.1%	12.2%
Rocky Mountain	3.2%	3.0%	-12.7%	-20.1%	13.2%	18.3%	9.6%	-0.4%
Pacific Coast	-10.3%	-4.3%	-32.8%	-46.6%	15.2%	21.4%	9.7%	30.6%
National	-4.8%	-2.6%	-10.5%	-14.3%	10.3%	17.4%	-2.9%	12.2%

[a] We used linear interpolation to generate 1996 and 2006 projected estimates from 1995, 2000, and 2010 data in Bowker and others (1999).

Hunting—Regional

For all hunting, the 1996-2006 period saw a decline in the number of participants in each Region, with a significant 33 percent decline in the Pacific Coast Region and nonsignificant declines in the Rocky Mountain (-13 percent), North (-7 percent), and South (-6 percent) Regions (Table 6). In projections from the last RPA Assessment, Bowker and others (1999) anticipated declines in all Regions except the Rocky Mountain Region (Table 10). While declines in the North, Rocky Mountain, and Pacific Coast Regions were all larger than projected in the last RPA Assessment, the South showed a smaller than projected decline (decrease of 6 percent compared to a 12 percent projected decline) (Table 10). FHWAR data showed no significant changes in days spent hunting (1996 to 2006) in the North, South, and Rocky Mountain Regions, but showed a larger, significant decrease in the Pacific Coast Region (Table 6). In contrast, Bowker and others (1999) projected a decrease in days in the South and Pacific Coast Regions, stable days in the North, and a slight increase in the Rocky Mountain Region (Table 10).

Regional patterns also varied by type of hunting activity over the past ten years. Since the 2000 RPA Assessment, small game hunting has seen larger declines in the North, South, and Pacific Coast Regions and a smaller, nonsignificant decline in the Rocky Mountain Region (Table 6, Figure 5). The total number of days spent small game hunting declined in all Regions, with the greatest drop in the Pacific Region (more than 50 percent decrease). The average number of days that each hunter devoted to small game hunting has remained relatively stable (Table 4). Over the same time period, participants in migratory bird hunting significantly decreased in the North, Pacific Coast, and Rocky Mountain Regions, with only the South remaining stable. Total number of days devoted to migratory birds hunting also remained stable in the South (Figure 6c). Number of days spent hunting migratory birds per participant each year grew in the South from 1996 to 2006 while all other Regions showed declines (Table 4). Since the 2000 RPA Assessment, the number of participants in big game hunting declined significantly in the Pacific Coast but remained stable in the North, South, and Rocky Mountain Regions. The total number of days devoted to big game hunting remained stable in all Regions except the Pacific Coast, where number of days declined. At the participant level, annual days spent big game hunting per person continued to grow.

Wildlife watching—National

Nationally, participation in away from home wildlife watching remained stable from 1996 to 2006, with a nonsignificant 3 percent decline in participants and a nonsignificant increase in number of days spent recreating. FHWAR reported that total number of days grew by 12 percent from 1996 to 2006, a nonsignificant increase. In contrast, Bowker and others (1999) projected a 10.3 percent increase in wildlife watching participants from 1996 through 2006 and a 17 percent increase in total days using data from the National Survey on Recreation and the Environment (Table 10). Total amount spent on wildlife watching away from home grew from 1996 to 2006 by $7.4 billion, with expenditures stable at approximately $31 billion in 2001 and 2006 (Table 8).

Wildlife watching—Regional

When examining Regional wildlife watching since 1996, only the Pacific Coast and the Rocky Mountain Regions showed growing numbers of participants, although both total days and days per participant increased in all Regions except the Rocky Mountain Region. The only statistically significant change in days and number of participants was the 12 percent decrease in wildlife watching participants in the North (Table 6). In comparison, forecasts from the last RPA Assessment predicted growth in wildlife watching participants and days in each Region, with the slowest growth in the North, and higher, similar levels of growth in the other three Regions (Bowker and others 1999) (Table 10). The actual patterns of growth observed in the Rocky Mountain and Pacific Coast Regions were smaller than predicted, and participation in the South declined by 6 percent (rather than growing by 14 percent as predicted). Participation in the North was predicted to grow by 6 percent but instead declined by 12 percent. Total number of days spent recreating in the North and South were also predicted to grow (Table 10) and did but at lower rates than predicted. The Rocky Mountain Region was predicted to grow in total number of days by 18 percent but instead remained stable. In contrast, the Pacific Coast Region had the highest predicted growth in number of days (21 percent) and surpassed that prediction with its 31 percent increase in the number of days participants devoted to wildlife watching.

Conclusion

Due to both economic and ecological impacts of changing wildlife recreation trends, understanding the ongoing changes in wildlife watching and hunting is essential if resource managers are to adjust their management goals and structures. The United States has a long history of wildlife-based recreation, but these recreation patterns are shifting. Although the United States retains a larger number of hunters than Canada, Australia, and the 35 European Union affiliated countries combined (Sharp and Wollscheid 2009), hunting participation is declining in the United States, except for big game hunting. Only 5.5 percent of Americans over the age of 16 hunt wildlife, and only 10 percent watch wildlife away from the home.

Over time, the numbers of hunters and wildlife watchers away from home have declined, but data suggest that between 2001 and 2006, the decline was tempered in some categories. For example, declines in all hunting, small game, and wildlife watching all showed less declining trends from 2001 to 2006 than in prior surveys. Migratory bird watching was an exception, with a steeper decline between 2001 and 2006 following a period of stability from 1996 to 2001. The average days each participant devoted to an activity remained stable or increased for nearly all activities, with the biggest increases seen in big game hunting and nonresidential wildlife watching. With the decline in the number of participants, there have been some decreases in total expenditures, although hunters are still spending the same total amount per participant from 1996 to 2006, and the amount spent per participant per day was stable since 1991. In contrast, nonresidential wildlife watchers are spending more per day and per person to watch wildlife in 2006 than they were 10 years previously, although the number of participants remained stable during this time.

We also note that, as a survey that focuses on primary recreation participation, FHWAR may differ from other assessments, such as the NSRE, in part because NSRE includes all reported instances of recreation (not just primary purpose) (Schuett and others 2009). The most recent update to the NSRE reported that in 2005 to 2009 (the most recent period of estimates), 20.9 million people hunted big game (9 percent of the U.S. population), 16.5 million hunted small game (7 percent of the U.S. population), and 4.9 million hunted migratory birds (2.1 percent of the U.S. population) (Cordell 2012). In all cases, these estimates were increases from or consistent with NSRE estimates from 1999 to 2001 but had declined since the mid 1990s. Therefore, while the estimates of number of participants were larger for each category in comparison to FHWAR survey results, overall trends since the 1990s were fairly similar.

Understanding the availability of land for recreation is often considered a key part of changing patterns of wildlife recreation; access for hunting, in particular, is considered a constraint on hunter participation (Kilgore and others 2008; Stedman and others 2008). Our results show that, over time, hunters are relying more exclusively on private land and that costs associated with private land leasing and owning have increased. Public land fees for hunting are less expensive and more stable over time, but public lands are distributed unevenly over the United States with far more land available in the West. However, while public land area in the eastern United States is smaller, the larger number of participants there means that these lands receive considerable numbers of hunting visits. Wildlife watching away from home also relies primarily on public lands across the United States, with a proportionally larger number of recreationists per land area of public land in the eastern United States. For both hunting and wildlife watching, as housing development and habitat loss on private land continues (Robles and others 2008; Stein and others 2010; USDA Forest Service 2012), it will be important to better understand the relationships between public and private land access for recreation, health of wildlife populations on public and private lands, and continued participation in wildlife-associated recreation.

Reviewing FHWAR results from the past four surveys available shows that despite any minor, and likely short-term, deviations from the longer-term pattern of declining participation in wildlife-associated recreation, the American public's ties to nature and its perceptions about sport hunting are changing. Demographic studies of wildlife hunting suggest that changes may accelerate in the future as the baby boom generation "ages out" of hunting (Winkler and Klaas 2011). Changes in hunting activity can have far-reaching impacts on wildlife communities, as declining harvests and shifting habitat management strategies can substantially impact wildlife populations and broader ecosystems (Manfredo and others 2009). At the same time, human participation in recreation depends upon the health of wildlife populations (Miller and Vaske 2003).

As wildlife recreation participation changes, the rationale and funding for wildlife management is also changing. Wildlife management in North America has relied on revenues and political support from hunters since the mid Nineteenth Century (Mahoney and Cobb 2010). The trends reported here provide evidence that concerns about a declining revenue base are justified. The number of primary participants in recreational hunting is not only declining in absolute terms but is also declining more rapidly relative to a growing American population with an increasingly diverse mix of values and attitudes toward wildlife. Numerous education programs are now geared toward bolstering participation and recruitment in wildlife-associated recreation (Enck and others 2000; Williams 2010). However, it seems that relying on license fees and excise taxes on hunting equipment as the primary funding mechanism supporting wildlife conservation in the United States will be insufficient to maintain a science-based management program in the future (Organ and others 2010). Broadening the funding sources to those who derive benefits from healthy wildlife communities, or impact wildlife resources, would help alleviate concerns for shrinking wildlife management budgets (Regan 2010). Meeting the funding challenge for wildlife conservation while accommodating the diversifying patterns of wildlife-based recreation will require new and flexible strategies in order to maintain both healthy wildlife populations and recreational opportunities in a changing America.

References

Aiken, R. 2009a. Net economic values of wildlife-related recreation in 2006: Addendum to the 2006 National Survey of Fishing, Hunting, and Wildlife-Associated Recreation. Report 2006-5. Washington, DC: Wildlife and Sport Fish Restoration Programs, U.S. Fish and Wildlife Service. 28 p.

Aiken, R. 2009b. Wildlife watching trends: 1991-2006. A reference report. Addendum to the 2006 National Survey of Fishing, Hunting, and Wildlife-Associated Recreation. Report 2006-3. Arlington, VA: U.S. Fish and Wildlife Service. 92 p.

Aiken, R. 2010. Trends in fishing and hunting 1991-2006: A focus on fishing and hunting by species. Addendum to the 2006 National Survey of Fishing, Hunting, and Wildlife-Associated Recreation. Report 2006-8. Arlington, VA: U.S. Fish and Wildlife Service. 68 p.

Bowker, J.M.; English, D.B.K.; Cordell, H.K. 1999. Projections of outdoor recreation participation to 2050. In: Cordell, H.K.; Betz, C.; Bowker, J.M.; [and others], eds. Outdoor recreation in American life: A national assessment of demand and supply trends. Champaign, IL: Sagamore Publishing: 323-351.

Bowker, J.M.; Askew, A.E.; Cordell, H.K.; Betz, C.J.; Zarnoch, S.J.; Seymour, L. 2012. Outdoor recreation participation in the United States—projections to 2060: a technical document supporting the Forest Service 2010 RPA Assessment. Gen. Tech. Rep. SRS-160. Ashville, NC: U.S. Department of Agriculture, Forest Service. 34 p.

Butler, J.S.; Shanahan, J.; Decker, D.J. 2003. Public attitudes toward wildlife are changing: A trend analysis of New York residents. Wildlife Society Bulletin 31: 1027-1036.

Cordell, H.K. 2012. Outdoor recreation trends and futures: A technical document supporting the Forest Service 2010 RPA assessment. Gen. Tech. Rep. SRS-150. Asheville, NC: U.S. Department of Agriculture, Forest Service, Southern Research Station. 167 p.

Cordell, H.K. 2004. Outdoor recreation for 21st Century America. A report to the nation: The national survey on recreation and the environment. State College, PA: Venture. 293 p.

Cortner, H.J.; Schweitzer, D.L. 1981. Institutional limits to national public planning for forest resources: the Resources Planning Act. Natural Resources Journal 21: 203-222.

de Groot, R.S.; Wilson, M.A.; Boumans, R.M.J. 2002. A typology for the classification, description and valuation of ecosystem functions, goods and services. Ecological Economics 41: 393-408.

Duffy, J.E. 2009. Why biodiversity is important to the functioning of real-world ecosystems. Frontiers in Ecology and the Environment 7: 437-444.

Enck, J.W.; Decker, D.J.; Brown, T.L. 2000. Status of hunter recruitment and retention in the United States. Wildlife Society Bulletin 28: 817-824.

English, D.B.K.; Kocis, S.M.; Zarnoch, S.J.; Arnold, J. R. 2002. Forest Service national visitor use monitoring process: Research method documentation. Gen. Tech. Rep. SRS-57. Asheville, NC: U.S. Department of Agriculture, Forest Service, Southern Research Station. 14 p.

Flather, C.H.; Brady, S.J.; Knowles, M.S. 1999. Wildlife resource trends in the United States: A technical document supporting the 2000 USDA Forest Service RPA assessment. Gen. Tech. Rep. RMRS-GTR-33. Fort Collins, CO: U.S. Department of Agriculture, Forest Service, Rocky Mountain Research Station. 79 p.

Froemke, P. 2011. Analysis of 2000 census data. Population proximity to National Forest System lands. Data on file with Miranda Mockrin at: U.S. Department of Agriculture, Forest Service, Rocky Mountain Research Station, Fort Collins, CO.

Jacobson, C.A.; Organ, J.F.; Decker, D.J.; Batcheller, G.R.; Carpenter, L. 2010. A conservation institution for the 21st Century: Implications for state wildlife agencies. Journal of Wildlife Management 74: 203-209.

Kilgore, M.A.; Snyder, S.A.; Schertz, J.M.; Taff, S.J. 2008. The cost of acquiring public hunting access on family forests lands. Human Dimensions of Wildlife 13: 175-186.

Leonard, J. 2008. Wildlife watching in the US: The economic impacts on national and state economies in 2006: Addendum to the 2006 National Survey of Fishing, Hunting, and Wildlife-Associated Recreation. Report 2006-1. Washington, DC: Wildlife and Sport Fish Restoration Programs, U.S. Fish and Wildlife Service. 12 p.

Loftus, A.J.; Flather, C.H. 2012. Fish and other aquatic resource trends in the United States: A technical document supporting the 2010 Forest Service RPA assessment. Gen. Tech. Rep. RMRS-GTR-283. Fort Collins, CO: U.S. Department of Agriculture, Forest Service, Rocky Mountain Research Station. 81 p.

Mahoney, S.P. 2009. Recreational hunting and sustainable wildlife use in North America. In: Dickson, B.; Hutton, J.; Adams, W.M., eds. Recreational Hunting, Conservation and Rural Livelihoods: Science and Practice. Oxford, England: Wiley-Blackwell: 266-281.

Mahoney, S.P.; Cobb, D. 2010. Future challenges to the model. Wildlife Professional 4(3): 83-85.

Manfredo, M.J.; Teel, T.L.; Henry, K.L. 2009. Linking society and environment: A multilevel model of shifting wildlife value orientations in the western United States. Social Science Quarterly 90: 407-427.

Mankin, P.C.; Warner, R.E.; Anderson, W.L. 1999. Wildlife and the Illinois public: A benchmark study of attitudes and perceptions. Wildlife Society Bulletin 27: 465-472.

Miller, C.; Vaske, J. 2003. Individual and situational influences on declining hunter effort in Illinois. Human Dimensions of Wildlife 8: 263-276.

Organ, J.F.; Mahoney, S.P.; Geist, V. 2010. Overview: The North American model. Wildlife Professional 4(3): 22-27.

Regan, R.J. 2010. Priceless, but not free: Why all nature lovers should contribute to conservation. Wildlife Professional 4(3): 39-41.

Robles, M.D.; Flather, C.H.; Stein, S.M.; Nelson, M.D.; Cutko, A. 2008. The geography of private forests that support at-risk species in the conterminous United States. Frontiers in Ecology and the Environment 6: 301-307.

Schuett, M.A; Warnick, R.B.; Lu, J. 2009. A qualitative analysis of national outdoor recreation surveys. Journal of Park and Recreation Administration 27(2): 46-49.

Sharp, R.; Wollscheid, K. 2009. An overview of recreational hunting in North America, Europe and Australia. In: Dickson, B.; Hutton, J.; Adams, W.M., eds. Recreational Hunting, Conservation and Rural Livelihoods. Oxford, England: Wiley-Blackwell: 25-38.

Southwick Associates. 2007. Hunting in America: An economic engine and conservation powerhouse. Association of Fish and Wildlife Agencies. 11 p.

Stedman, R.C.; Bhandari, P.; Luloff, A.E.; Diefenbach, D.R.; Finley, J.C. 2008. Deer hunting on Pennsylvania's public and private lands: A two-tiered system of hunters? Human Dimensions of Wildlife 13: 222-233.

Stein, S.M.; McRoberts, R.E.; Nelson, M.D.; [and others]. 2010. Private forest habitat for at-risk species: Where is it and where might it be changing? Journal of Forestry 108: 61-70.

Teel, T.L.; Manfredo, M.J. 2010. Understanding the diversity of public interests in wildlife conservation. Conservation Biology 24: 128-139.

U.S. Department of Agriculture. 2000. Summary report: 1997 National Resources Inventory (revised December 2000). Washington, DC: Natural Resources Conservation Service, and Ames, IA: Iowa State University, Statistical Laboratory. 90 p.

U.S. Department of Agriculture, Forest Service. 2012. Future scenarios: A technical document supporting the Forest Service 2010 RPA Assessment. Gen. Tech. Rep. RMRS-GTR-272. Fort Collins, CO: U.S. Department of Agriculture, Forest Service, Rocky Mountain Research Station. 34 p.

U.S. Department of the Interior, Fish and Wildlife Service; U.S. Department of Commerce, U.S. Census Bureau [USFWS and U.S. Census Bureau]. 2007. National Survey of Fishing, Hunting, and Wildlife-Associated Recreation. Arlington, VA: U.S. Fish and Wildlife Service. 164 p.

Walls, M.; Darley, S.; Siikamäki, J. 2009. The state of the great outdoors: America's parks, public lands, and recreation resources. Washington, DC: Resources for the Future. 97 p.

White, E.M.; Stynes, D.J. 2010. Spending profiles of National Forest visitors, National Visitor Use and Monitoring Program. Round 2 update. Unpublished report. Fort Collins, CO: U.S. Department of Agriculture, Forest Service. 38 p.

Williams, S. 2010. Wellspring of wildlif funding: How hunter and angler dollars fuel wildlife conservation. Wildlife Professional 4(3): 35-38.

Winkler, R.; Klaas, R. 2011. Declining deer hunters: Wisconsin's gun deer hunter numbers are continuing to decline. Madison, WI: University of Wisconsin, Applied Population Laboratory. 10 p.

Winter, S. 2011. Analysis of 2003-2008 National visitor use and monitoring program. Number of visits and type of visits to National Forest System lands. Data on file with Miranda Mockrin at: U.S. Department of Agriculture, Forest Service, Rocky Mountain Research Station, Fort Collins, CO.

Glossary_____

All definitions from National Survey of Fishing, Hunting, and Wildlife-Associated Recreation (USDI FWS and U.S. Census Bureau 2007).

Around-the-home wildlife watching—Activity within 1 mile of home with one of six primary purposes: (1) taking special interest in or trying to identify birds or other wildlife; (2) photographing wildlife; (3) feeding birds or other wildlife; (4) maintaining natural areas of at least 1/4 acre for the benefit of wildlife; (5) maintaining plantings (such as shrubs and agricultural crops) for the benefit of wildlife; and (6) visiting public land to observe, photograph, or feed wildlife. Also referred to as "residential wildlife watching."

Away-from-home wildlife watching—Trips or outings at least 1 mile from home for the primary purpose of observing, photographing, or feeding wildlife. Trips to zoos, circuses, aquariums, and museums are not included. Also referred to as "nonresidential wildlife watching."

Big game—Large mammal species and wild turkey hunted for sport or subsistence that can be native or desired non-native species that were intentionally introduced to provide hunting opportunities. Examples are bear, deer, elk, moose, feral pig, wild turkey, and similar large animals that are hunted.

Expenditures—Money spent during the year the National Survey of Fishing, Hunting, and Wildlife-Associated Recreation was conducted on wildlife-related recreational trips and equipment in the United States. Expenditures include money spent by a participant for themselves or the value of gifts received by a participant.

Home—The starting point of a wildlife-related recreational trip. It may be a permanent residence or a temporary or seasonal residence such as a cabin.

Migratory birds—Collectively referred to game birds that regularly migrate from one region or climate to another. Examples are waterfowl (ducks, geese, and swans), so-called "webless" migratory species such as mourning dove and woodcock, and other migratory birds that may be hunted.

Nonresidential wildlife watching—See "away-from-home wildlife watching" above.

Other animals—Coyotes, crows, foxes, groundhogs, prairie dogs, raccoons, and similar animals that can be legally hunted and are not classified as big game, small game, or migratory birds. These animals may be classified as unprotected or predatory by the state in which they are hunted. Feral pigs are classified as "other animals" in all states except Hawaii, where they are considered big game.

Participant—According to the National Survey of Fishing, Hunting, and Wildlife-Associated Recreation, participant is an individual who reported engaging in hunting or wildlife watching during the survey year.

Participation rate—The number of participants in a particular activity divided by the total population (that is, civilian, noninstitutionalized population 16 years old and older), as reported by the National Survey of Fishing, Hunting, and Wildlife-Associated Recreation.

Residential wildlife watching—See "around-the-home wildlife watching" above.

Small game—Small-bodied resident mammals and birds that can be native or desired non-native species that were intentionally introduced to provide hunting opportunities. Examples are grouse, pheasants, quail, rabbits, squirrels, and similar small animals for which states have established seasons and bag limits

www.ingramcontent.com/pod-product-compliance
Lightning Source LLC
Chambersburg PA
CBHW081132280526
45787CB00007B/3045